Escape from Hell
and
the Almighty White Guy with a Beard

James La Croce

A
J
O
U
R
N
E
Y

I
N
T
O

How I learned to stop worrying

and love the mystery

THE HEART OF SPIRITUAL

N
O
I
T
A
M
R
O
F
S
N
A
R
T

CPSIA information can be obtained
at www.ICGtesting.com
Printed in the USA
LVHW041452081120
671085LV00001B/197

For Mary, Mary, and Mary
My Sea of Love

For former students and parishioners
The occasion of many graces

For the monk and the marvelous maniacs

Trustworthy friends

You know who you are

Author's Note

My late-in-life escape
from the Almighty White Guy's hell
was nothing more than an escape
from a figment of the religious imagination.

But doing this was not easy.
And you may not like my exit strategy.
Then again, it may be just what you are looking for.

I give myself a shameless pat on the back,
with the help of Raymond Chandler:

"Do I read my stuff when published?
Yes, and at the very great risk of being called
an egotistical twerp. I find it damn hard to put down.
Even me, that knows all about it.
There must be some magic in the writing after all..."

Table of Contents

Overture: The Song of Songs ix

Preface: BUY THIS BOOK! xi

1. MY LONG DELAYED ESCAPE - I can explain it, I can tell you why 1

2. MY HAPPY OLD AGE - That must count for something 5

3. THE PRICE OF ESCAPING - Others paid more than I did 11

4. A BETTER ESCAPE ROUTE? - Saying no to Phil 17

5. FROM BROOKLYN TO PERU - A few laughs, a few graces 27

6. THE PERILS IN PERU (Fall 1971 – Winter 1972) - The Good News was the Bad News 38

7. BACK IN THE STATES (Winter 1972 – Spring 1977) - My trustworthy friends 71

8. THE CABIN IN THE WOODS (Winter 1972- Spring 1977) - Jesus the Nazarene 102

9. PARDON THE INTERRUPTION - Bad Uncle Jim 119

10. ON A CATHOLIC COLLEGE CAMPUS (Early 1980's) - The Son's divinity? - The Father's Hell? 126

11. ONE SUNDAY AT MASS (May, 1985) - I could not pray to God as 'Almighty' 166

12. THE VACATION INCIDENT (June, 1993) - A radical new experience of prayer 177

13. SURPRISED BY MY VIVID IMAGINATION (Late 1990's) - A short story and a tall tale...............................188

14. AT HOME PONDERING (2000- 2008) 201

15. FROM HERE TO ETERNITY - ?????????????????????????...231

Overture: The Song of Songs

THE GLORIFIED CHRIST SINGS:

Put the spotlight on me:

I am the answer to sin and error,

I am the Prince of Peace,

I am the only ticket to heaven,

I am the Savior of the world,

I am true God of true God and you better believe it.

THE HUMBLE NAZARENE SINGS:

Ease up, Big Guy in the sky:

The world still pines in sin and error,

There is no peace on earth,

There are other tickets to heaven,

(If God is love it cannot be otherwise)

Planet earth has yet to be "saved".

I am the fullest revelation of God.

  -in my hidden life of thirty years,

  -in my prayer about the kingdom on earth,

-in my ministry to the lowly and the mighty,

-in my near death parable about the least,

The spotlight is on the least Big Guy:

In them God's name will be made holy;

In them is the salvation of the world.

Preface: BUY THIS BOOK!

I believe I am qualified to write this book about God and Son. I have lived with them for over seventy years- as a boy and a man, a layman in the pew and a priest in the pulpit, a celibate and a married man (with church permission), a man with authority and a man opposed to authority, a man who once gloried in the right answers (I have a doctorate in Sacred Theology) and a man whose final comfort is in his questions (I have this book as evidence).

From 1950 to 1970 I was a seminary student and a priest. From 1970 to 1980 I was an anti-poverty and anti-war activist. (I remember those years as "my life on the road" with Jesus). From 1980 to 2000 I taught Religious Studies in a Roman Catholic College and in 2000 I retired as Professor Emeritus. From 2000 until God knows when I have been pondering.

My pondering led to questions and doubts which I came to call "Rude Awakenings". I called them "Awakenings" because only now was I becoming aware that I could escape the fear of hell and the image of God as the almighty white guy with a beard, making threats and promising rewards. I called my questions "Rude" because they were offensive to pious ears, and, at times, even to mine.

God help me if I give the impression I am writing to you from high moral ground when I write about my ten years as an activist against war and for the poor. I gave only a decade of my life trying to put down the mighty by living with and working with the lowly. And I did so on the cheap. I just happened to be an angry celibate forty year old man at a time when my anger could be harnessed to religious and political movements that dominated the 1970's in North and South America. I was always on the fringe of this mighty saga. But the saga did not remain on the fringe of me. Thus this book about God and Son.

Where am I taking you? Why am I taking you there? How am I going to take you there? What kind of rude questions am I asking?

Where am I taking you?

I am taking you where pious believers fear to tread – where peace and justice mean more than heaven and hell; where God as "the mystery" means more than God as "the almighty"; where questions about God and Son are revered more than the so-called answers.

The questions are rude:

1. Why is God not an almighty presence on our planet?
2. Why is the Son so unlike the Father?
3. Why always with the creeds when we worship?
   Why not "Lord, we believe, help our unbelief"?
4. Why do we not sing "Nobody knows God's name"?

Why am I taking you there?

Planet earth will not be well served by Christianity in the cliff-hanging third millennium of the Christian calendar if Christians continue to live mostly by what John 3:16 says about God and Son at the expense of what Luke 4:18 tells us.

In 3:16 John quotes himself. He would have us believe God so loved the world that he sent Jesus to save only those who believed in Jesus.

In 4:18 Luke quotes Jesus who would have us believe that God so loved the world that he sent Jesus to serve those for whom life is a bitch and then it ends.

You should know that bible quotes are part of a sacred story not of a precise history. Thus the difference in what Jesus supposedly said about his mission and what John supposedly said about Jesus' mission.

The world in the third millennium needs more Luke 4:18 Christians than it does John 3:16 Christians. It needs Christians who believe Jesus was sent to do something wonderful for planet earth not to save only those who believe in him and let the others and the planet go to hell. It needs Christians who believe it is by living the Luke text that a follower of Jesus takes up the cross of Jesus. It needs more Jesus believers who take seriously the last parable of Jesus: depart from me you accursed sinner for when I was hungry you did not see the hungry one as me.

Jesus' parable on judgment is not a proof of the existence of hell but proof that Jesus was madder than hell when about to be crucified. He had been knocking himself out for the least and they were still not being treated as if they were Jesus. Worse yet, his mission to them was about to be stopped. The feet that took him to the least and the hands that fed and healed them were soon to be nailed to two planks of wood. That's when he lost his temper and told the parable about hell. Christianity needs believers who believe Jesus is still madder than hell that the least on planet earth are not treated as if they were Jesus.

The community of Jesus has always and everywhere lacked the ardor and tenacity of the ministry of Jesus to the wretched and huddling masses. Belief in treating them as if they were Jesus is not a belief included in any of the Christian creeds. A Christian must believe in God as almighty, in Jesus as divine, in the resurrection of the dead but not in treating the least as if they were Jesus.

The words of Jesus have been about as effective as those of the Statue of Liberty: "Give me your tired, your poor, your huddled masses yearning to breathe free, the wretched refuse of your teeming shore. Send these, the homeless, tempest-tossed to me. I lift my lamp beside the golden door."

If things have not been going well for humanity on planet earth you can figure it out for yourselves.

How will I take you to where I want to take you?
I write as a friend talking to friends. But I do not rely on the day to day language I use with friends. Writing a book is like writing in another language. One must use words and put sentences together in a way that will hold the attention of countless readers. My words and sentences add up to a light hearted, heavy-handed, and devoutly devastating swipe at long held traditions about God and Son. That should hold your attention.

I rely heavily on stories about my personal experiences with God and Son. There is nothing more powerful than a story to make a point. That is why the bible is so popular.
It is a book of stories based on the religious experiences of two communities who have earned the respect and reverence of countless millions down through the centuries.

What kind of rude questions am I asking?

1. When reciting the creed at Sunday worship should I profess my faith in God only as "the Father" and only as "the Almighty"?

Look where this restriction has taken us. We have come to imagine God mostly as an all-powerful white man with a beard who knows when we've been good or bad and who has prepared a cruel and unforgiving punishment for those who are bad. That's as almighty as almighty can get!

There is something unseemly about God as proclaiming "power is my name, power is my game." That belief reminds me of a cartoon in *The New Yorker*. It shows an elderly white man with a beard about to hurl a bolt of lightning from heaven. Three females, "the Zeusettes", are singing: "He's got a fist full of lightnin' and he's gonna cut loose! He's the man with a plan! He's the cat they call Zeus."

As a nation under the image of God as the Almighty we anointed 'the bomb' as our almighty prince of peace: "We got a fist full of lightnin' and we are ready to cut loose". But now the

Prince has lost its power to protect us. Now we are more vulnerable than ever.

Other nations under God as the Almighty are waging war more and more in the name of God and less and less in the name of national sovereignty. It had wrongly been assumed that the modern world had put an end to that nonsense.

2. Must I imagine God as almost always angry about something or other? Should I relate to God as being "touchy" about what my Church insists are wrong beliefs and bad behavior? Don't these hurt us more than they hurt God? Shouldn't God feel anguish and concern about our "sins" rather than anger? Why should masturbation, missing mass, or membership in the wrong community of faith send anyone to hell? Have we fashioned an image of a God who has such poor self esteem, such a fragile ego that "He" so easily feels "offended" by what we do or fail to do? Being that touchy would make life as miserable for God as it is for us.

Being quick to anger and harsh in punishment sounds like bad parenting to me. That image of God calls to mind the sign I saw posted in a diner in Maine: "The beatings will continue until morale improves."

3. Is it wrong to imagine God as "Love Unstoppable"? Any public attempt to do that has always been condemned as a heresy. And yet, even given free will, is it not a pious probing to imagine divine love as a weapon of mass seduction? Is it not true piety to imagine that the power of divine love is the mystery? Is it not an act of faith and hope to imagine that God has a way of taking care of justice without resorting to eternal unforgiveness and everlasting pain? Just because there was a Hitler does not mean there has to be a hell.

4. Does justice without hell sound too wishy-washy? Would you say then that the only thing that keeps belief in heaven from being wishy-washy is the belief that you get there and I don't, or vice-versa? Should we thank God for our belief in hell since it helps us believe in heaven without being seen as being wishy-washy? Now there's a worrisome thought.

Here's a scary thought. If hell was first populated by angels who were kicked out of heaven what security do we have in heaven?

This is even scarier. If God is an all-loving Father and if hell is as advertised then God as the architect and CEO of hell must be the most miserable S.O.B. who ever lived. Why would the CEO of hell insist that we call him "Father"?

5. Does God as advertised, have a list of hell-worthy sins? Why do not all faiths follow the same list? Suppose two women, one catholic and the other protestant, both practicing birth control, are both killed instantly in a car accident. Does the catholic go to hell while the protestant goes to heaven? Or do they both go to hell but only the protestant is surprised?

6. Why does Christian preaching and teaching on hell not feature Jesus' last parable, told shortly before his death? It was Jesus' final version of what to expect at judgment time. Jesus was a man about to die, and not merely posing as a man about to die. His parable was for himself as well as his listeners: "I am ready to face my father in heaven. I treated the least as if they were me."

How can his last parable count for so little?

In asking these very rude questions I am reminded of the cartoon showing a preacher in the pulpit announcing to the congregation: "No sermon for you today. You are all going to hell anyway."

My questions are not expressions of disdain for mother Church. I would be a liar if I said I am not proud of her vigorous intellectual life and am not moved by her ancient rituals- especially her liturgical chants (words by King David and music by Pope Gregory). And I would be an ungrateful wretch if I did not confess that without mother Church I would not have had my long and rewarding life with God. She made it possible for me to become a devout believer in a divine presence and a divine good will at work in my life. Indeed, it may be that I can write this book only because my church raised me in a way that makes writing this book possible. As a wise philosopher once noted: "One repays a teacher badly if one always remains a pupil."

I am not a religious idealist. I know the sins of my church as well as her enemies. But I do not sing their song: "'Tis a pity she's a whore." I can live with the sins of my mother, even those of the fetid fourteenth century when she was more an agent of corruption than of sanctification. I have even learned to live with her centuries of harping that she was the only true Church.

I can live with the weaknesses of my mother the church, except the one lamented in this book: 'Tis a pity her doctrines and rituals give so much to God as all mighty and so little to God as all mystery, and so much to Jesus as "the Christ" and so little to Jesus as "the Nazarene".

I am not a rationalist bigot. In questioning the reverence given to God as an almighty presence I do not suggest that God never cures a cancer. I do say cures will almost never, if ever, be done by God as an almighty show-off. There are no Divine "Ta-dahs!" No restoring legs blasted to bits by roadside bombs. That is not going to happen. I am at peace with my belief that it is not an almighty presence but a hidden godly presence we should revere, love and cherish, day in and day out. I believe it is the holy will of God not to be present to us as "the almighty".

I am not a flaming liberal. I know that our stories and beliefs about the risen and glorified Christ have given and are giving peace and joy to countless millions. I was one of them for most of my life. I too lived my life of faith revering the Christ for what he can do for me. For me, the good that Jesus did in his road ministry had been interred with his bones.

I am not an ex-Catholic or former Catholic. I am a retired Roman Catholic. The meager pension that keeps my faith alive is provided by the Nazarene's road ministry to the kingdom on earth.

I am a man of faith who in good faith reveres his questions and doubts. They reflect my determination to make my faith as honest, straightforward, and personal as possible.

Believe me; I can understand if you do not want to go where my "Rude Awakenings" take you. I was in my fifties before I dared to go there and decided to stay there. Only in my seventies was I ready to publish the story of my religious experience of God and Son.

I almost did not publish this book because of the fear of going to hell if I shared my questions and doubts with others. I decided not to give into that fear. That decision may seem foolish. It is foolish. Where eternal damnation is at stake it seems best to play it safe, as is the custom among pious and not so pious believers.

But I have no choice. Like any serious believer I am moved not just to keep the faith but share it – even more so having been a priest and professor. It will not be too long before I meet God. If God is all-knowing, as advertised, "He" already knows what is in my heart, what I have put in writing, what I am determined to publish. When we meet, face to face so to speak, I have no choice but to tell the truth, the whole truth, and nothing but the truth. Faking it before God will do me no good whatsoever.

There is no use moaning and groaning or quaking and shaking about the rude questions I am asking. In fact, I take great comfort in the two gospel accounts which have Jesus dying with a very rude question on his lips: "My God, my God, why have you forsaken me?" (Yes, rude questions can be prayers). I am no Jesus but as a follower I cannot be faulted for taking heart in these two gospel accounts of the very last words of Jesus.

Permission to publish:

I would not give myself permission to publish this book about God if I believed God had written a book about God. Or if I believed God had an obviously godly hand in the biblical books about God – as in the kind of hand that could make two instant adults. I believe God was behind the making of the bible as much as he was behind the making of the universe – way behind.

Nor would I write this book about God if I felt obligated to refer to God, a pure spirit, always and only as a male. I usually refer to God as "He" only because it is customary. Even today, in our progressive culture, it is still not O.K. to refer to God as "She." I personally believe that in referring to the incomprehensible divine presence in our life "mother" is as good as "father", "breast" is as good as "rock", "tears" are as good as "fire", "womb" is as good as "fortress"- and yes, "pubic triangle" is as good as the "traditional triangle" that for far too long has highlighted God as a masculine presence among us.

We should not reinforce the decisions of the men who run our church even though we obey them for the common good.

Some practical matters:

1. PRAYER:

While at prayer, should we not try harder to love our enemies? Should we ever ask for God's help in killing them when things have gotten out of hand and the killing machine has been unleashed?

While at prayer, should we not try harder to be practical? Does it not make sense to pray for leaders here and abroad who do not talk and act like a Louis L'Amour cowboy, leaders who are quick to boast: "I'll handle the shovel that puts dirt on your grave and the gun that puts you there"? Now more than ever do we not need leaders who are not trigger-happy?

Google "The War Prayer" by Mark Twain. That should help you in your prayers.

2. WAR:

In the Big Picture, Warriors go into battle willing to die for the defense of the nation that sent them there.

In the Little Picture, those in the field of fire do not always have such noble sentiments. They die in self-defense and in defense of their comrades – especially in a war that is suspect and controversial.

In my lifetime our country fought in two wars that were vastly unpopular with many if not most of its citizens. Both were fought because of over zealous and misguided reactions by our leaders due mostly to wrongly placed threats to national security. And that is putting it kindly. What kind of a democracy is this if that dire situation continues?

Our country no longer professes to believe that slavery, segregation, and sexism are OK with God and Son. When will it bite the bullet on militarism? It is time to take a closer look at war, at the way we assume war is inevitable, at the way we fight our wars, at the reasons we go to war. Have we been O.K. with God on all counts? It is time to begin to imagine a world without war. It is time to confess that even mother earth suffers our violence. Is it not true that in this we are without shame?

3. JESUS:

Why has Jesus' birthday hymn "Peace on earth" not put an end to war? What could the angels at Bethlehem have been thinking? Silly song! What do angels know about life on planet earth?

Why has Jesus' kingdom prayer for "daily bread" not put an end to hunger? What could Jesus have been thinking in praying for food for all, food worthy of Our Father's table? Silly man! Or was he? Did he believe something we have not yet learned to believe?

4. OUR TROOPS:

Does "Support our troops" only and always mean "Support our war"? Is such a claim a graceless deception? Most likely many of our troops would prefer we get them out of this war. No doubt, the Support Slogan, though it may serve to kill more troops, gives comfort to those who want to be assured that a loved one's body or some of its parts were not given "in vain". This kind of pain killer reminds me of the oft-used pain killer given to parents when a child dies "in vain" – as in a five year old girl run over by a cement truck while riding her new birthday bicycle: "It is the will of God."

Not that there is anything wrong with these pain killers. Any piety that can help anyone get through the dark night of despair is O.K. by me – even if it prolongs a war or puts God's good name in a bad light. But to take one pain killer as patriotism and the other as theology is an abomination before God and country. I would suggest that the "Patriots" who chant "Support our Troops" read Walt Whitman on the Civil War:

> "I saw battle-corpses, myriads of them....
> But I saw they were not as was thought,
> They themselves were fully at rest, they suffer'd not,
> ... the armies that remain'd suffer'd."

4. OUR WORSHIP:

While at worship, whether we worship on Friday, Saturday or Sunday, should we not try to be humble? When the going gets tough have not each of the three great Revelation Religions given good reason for doubting their boasts about being highly favored by God? Israel and Islam have made the land of milk and honey a land of blood and gore. Christianity has long been divided against itself and has helped shape a nation that is much better at bombing nations than baptizing them. What's that all about?

5. THE ALMIGHTY:

Should we revere God as "The Almighty" if God is clearly determined to let the chips fall where they may? No Rabbi was sent by God to threaten Hitler as in the story of Moses threatening Pharaoh: "Let my people go – or else." Our post 9/11 nation, still struggling with racism and sexism, will not be blessed with an African-American devout Muslim immigrant woman sent by God to be our unifying president. Such mighty signs would make the case that God wants to be revered as "The Almighty". That case has yet to be made, except, of course, in our sacred stories.

6. GOOD FRIDAY:

Why is the Friday on which Jesus was crucified called "Good"? Is it because we favor the story that tells us that while Friday was bad for Jesus it was good for us, that the whips and nails which opened his body at that very moment opened the gates of heaven, saved sinners?

Another story suggests Jesus died fighting for the little guys against the big guys – suggesting that Friday should be called BAD Friday because the big guys won that battle and because that Friday was bad both for Jesus and for us.

7. GRANDCHILDREN:

While talking to your grandchildren about religion, try to be cautious, especially after reading this book. While writing it I was very cautious when my eight year old granddaughter called me on the phone.

Grandpa Jim, how did religion get started?

She still believed in Adam, Eve, and Santa. I could not tell her all three were fictional. So I shared with her a word-picture that went something like this:

Imagine yourself in a world with very few people, and everyone lives out in the open, almost like animals. It is a lonely world. You hardly know how to talk and there are very few people to talk to and they are scattered all over the place. It is a hard world to live in. You know very little about getting food or making clothes or building shelter. It is a scary world to live in. You are afraid of the dark, the cold, floods, fire, lightning, earthquakes, wild animals and dreams. It is an awesome world to look at – with its sun, moon, stars, mountains and oceans. It is a mysterious world to live in – for it gives freely and takes away just as freely. Who or what is behind this giving and this taking? How powerful they or it must be. How can we get their help and appease their anger? Eventually "help from above" was called God and belief in that help was called religion. God loving us and our loving God as well as one another was believed to be the highest form of religion.

Some day my granddaughter will, I trust, learn to see the Adam and Eve story in light of my explanation. Hopefully, it will not be too rude of an awakening for her, that she will learn to read the bible as a book of stories not of facts.

Now, on to the story of my life with God and Son.

This is my story and I'm sticking to it.

1. MY LONG DELAYED ESCAPE -

I can explain it, I can tell you why

In the 1930's and 1940's our nuns, catechism, and bible had me believing that there was no escape from the threat of hell. Threatening us was part of God's job. Take away the threat and everyone would end up in hell. God knows, we are all sinners. God goes about being God Almighty primarily by way of this threat. If not for that he would be a lesser God. God's goodness I was taught, day in and day out, is wrapped in "his" almighty power – the power to reward and punish not for just a trillion years, but forever – and ever.

God gets the God-job done by judging every thought, word and deed. He goes by "the book" and by whatever "the pope" says. Forget goblins, children, you now have God to contend with.

The nuns were convincing teachers. I can vouch for that. Their text book, The Baltimore Catechism, gave us age-appropriate information about how God went about his business. The simple questions and pat answers were reassuring. Just do as instructed and there will be nothing to worry about. The fact that we were so well informed was the bright side about the dark side of this teaching. It was a big part of the satisfaction of being a Catholic. The nuns, priests, bishop and Pope saw to it that I knew exactly how God goes about being God on planet earth. Pound for pound my church has more doctrines and dogmas about God and how God goes about being God than any other religion.

Was there a world to be made? If so, the creator made it all by himself in six days. Was the world filled with sinners who needed to be saved? If so, it was because the creator had the power to mark each soul with sin and the power to let Satan loose to go about seeking whom he may devour. Did he save these sinners? If so, it was only those who repented their sins, told them to the priest in confession, and received the sacraments regularly.

The Father made the world out of nothing. The Son saved the world by his blood. The spirit sanctifies the world by his grace. Without grace we are nothing, can do nothing. We are powerless, God is all-powerful.

I had my questions of course. Why was I born with sin on my soul? Where is the soul in my body? (I pictured it as a filmy white blob near the heart). Why did God weaken my will and darken my intellect? Why does God allow Satan to tempt me?

The priests and nuns told me God did this so he could come through with flying colors and save me. That's what God likes to do best. The fact that the priests and nuns wore "uniforms" helped a lot. Uniforms add the weight of authority.

I will always be grateful to the nuns. They taught me under the most difficult circumstances. The classes were large and they had very little in the way of creature comforts. Their colleagues in the Public Schools would have gone on strike if ordered to work under their conditions. They paid for the fact that our parents paid nothing for our education.

I will not romanticize how the nuns did their job. "I'll put the fear of God into you" was a common threat in our schools. Today's children would be badly served by the fear tactics and physical discipline of those times. Teachers today would be arrested for what some of the nuns did in the way of physical punishment. Not that they were cruel. They handled discipline in school as our parents did at home. More to the point, they handled it as God does. God's reliance on the threat and the punishment of hell was as solid a vote as possible for the spiritual value of threats and physical punishment. I trusted God, my parents, the nuns. I took fear and discipline in stride. Today I see these things differently, as does the law.

Still, I count my experience with the nuns as a plus. They handed down what they received as they received it, as is the custom in a believing community. They gave me a free education when times were tough. I thank God for them. It would be wrong to condemn them on the basis of what we know today. Doing that has always been a deadly pleasure.

I spent about twenty-five years in church classrooms. Only orthodox Jews spent more time in religion classes than I did. I was taught that a correct knowledge of how God goes about being God is not only a possibility but an obligation. That is why God gave us an inerrant bible and infallible teachers. God is, above all, "teacher" of the mysteries. God is, above all, "touchy" and even "nasty" about incorrect forms of belief and worship.

And that, my friends, is why it took me so long to learn to stop worrying and love the mystery, to escape from hell and the almighty white guy with a beard.

My awakening, though it came late in life, has helped me enjoy a happy old age. And what a blessing that has turned out to be.

2. MY HAPPY OLD AGE -

That must count for something

I could not write this book if I were not so blessed in my old age. There is no doubt about that. I cannot characterize my old age as anything but the greatest of graces.

Psalm 70 has been sung and answered. "Do not cast me off in the time of my old age; do not forsake me when my strength is spent."

I am 78 years old and I am doing quite well. Much has been given me and little has been taken away. I move under my own power. I enjoy the food and drink my diminished income allows. I have been blessed with good genes and when I turned 70 I was doubly blessed in having a physician who was attentive, open-minded and up to date in her discipline. A half hour with her, which she always gave me, had a placebo effect on me. When I turned 77 I dodged the cancer bullet, thanks to my cautious and capable doctor. He spotted the bullet while it was still a pellet. Thanks to that woman and that man I may die in good health, with, of course, the emphasis on "may". Such grace or good luck cannot be assumed.

I no longer have to "earn" my living. I am not pressured by clocks and calendars, deadlines and meetings, the lure of lecturing and the stress of lecturing. My sense of myself is more solid than it ever has been. More than ever I am at peace with the courage of my convictions. How others see me is still important to me but not in the debilitating way it had been in the past.

Even though I am more and more out of the circle of my colleagues, family and friends, I am never bored. I still value the social scene. I still enjoy the pleasure of being with those who know how to party. I find satisfaction in sharing time with family and friends. I am highly energized when I'm with others who are doing some good in the world. But I do not lament my diminished presence in society. Truth-be-told I have never been happier. And that was even before I became pregnant, even before my promiscuous pondering gave birth to a book. My wife will verify that.

My wife is, of course, one of the three Mary's to whom this book is dedicated. She and I are together because we each took a risk which demanded courage. Separately we endured a painful uprooting of life as we had known it – me from the priesthood and she from marriage. Each of us believed it was the right thing to do. At the time we did not know these separate decisions would bring us together – and that we would be married with the blessing of our Church. Before blessing us the Church "reduced me to the lay state" and "annulled" her marriage. To be "reduced" and "annulled" meant that our respective decisions, once suspect, were now permitted. I was reduced and she was annulled, each separately and quietly and without ritual celebration. The terms "reduced" and "annulled" muted the grace of our decisions. But our risk-taking proved to be a great grace. My wife and I still cling to one another as one flesh. Our nakedness is not a shame but a blessing. We are bread and wine to one another in the sacrament of marriage. We can be, at times, a couple of thorn birds, but less and less so rather than more and more. We have been especially blessed in bearing with grace the pains of intimacy. Our life together may be our greatest grace. At least it seems so to us in our experience of remaining two while becoming one and in the growing realization that we were meant to face death together. We look forward to singing Paul's song: "Death, where is thy sting?" How many of us, even those who are pious believers, can sing that song when it really counts? Everyone wants to get to heaven but no one wants to die to get there. Very few of us think of death as a grace we do not deserve. At the hour of death many give into dread rather than opening up to the great expectations so often and so cheaply proclaimed.

Each day is a gift, a gift I treasure. There are, of course, some minuses in my life, as is the custom on planet earth. But my life as a whole is still a plus, not yet a minus. My life with God is full of grace.

My spiritual life has become more private, personal and solitary. I take to heart the words of the respected philosopher A.N. Whitehead: "Religion is what we do with our solitariness." Why not? I will go to God alone. I may as well learn to be comfortable with God, one on one. Old age is a blessing in that my time alone increases little by little. Old age helps me adjust to being alone, being at peace with myself, being ready for that meeting in which I will be alone with God.

Old age is a time for listening more and more to the "personal voice" of God and less and less to the "public voice" heard in the scriptures and sermons. For the elderly every other piety is peripheral to that of being attentive to the personal voice of God. And, as you know, that is a difficult piety to come by and live by.

But I dare not give up. I believe that it is my turn to be picked up, fondled and silently whispered to. I believe that the "God-Shepherd" is being especially attentive to me, an elderly lamb now being separated from the flock by reason of longevity. It is high time for me to listen attentively to the sound of divine silence.

In my listening to the silent voice of God I have learned a few things that surprised me. One of them is that I cannot take pride in being a believer. Belief was handed to me on a silver platter. I am not a self-made believer. I have no reason to boast. I could be tempted to boast if my grandparents, parents, uncles, aunts, and cousins were all agnostics or atheists instead of believers. I might feel like boasting if there had been a strong atheist or agnostic voice in my school, in the town newspaper, on the radio (we had no T.V.), in the movies, in the pool rooms, bowling alleys, and dance halls of my youth. Belief in God was spoon fed to me the moment I was able to take such nourishment. I am not complaining, mind you, but I dare not boast or fuss about being a believer. Truth be told, I do not even look down on or criticize those whose beliefs differ from mine. Nor does the God I have come to believe in. That God is more grounded in common sense and a sense of fair play than the religions would have us believe. To me it is sheer nonsense and borders on blasphemy to believe otherwise. If I had been born and raised as a Protestant or a Muslim that is most likely what I would be today. Statistics on conversions make that evident. I cannot believe that one is deprived of God's love and grace or receives less in the way of love and grace by accident of birth.

Each day of my old age is a gift, a gift I treasure. My life with God is full of grace.

3. THE PRICE OF ESCAPING -

Others paid more than I did

Every escape begins with a first step. No matter how small the step it is always the most crucial step. I took my first step in the Spring of 1971. I did not know it was the first step in my escape from hell and the almighty white Guy, but it was.

I was forty years old. I had been ordained a priest in Rome, earned a doctorate in Sacred Theology at the Pontifical Gregorian University, had worked as assistant chancellor in the Bishop's office, and was now the happy pastor of Holy Family Parish, a suburban parish in Harrisburg, Pa. Bill, an assistant to the Bishop, lived with me in the parish rectory and helped out in parish work as much as he could. He had also studied in Rome and was about my age. We were close friends.

I remember well the twenty-two words that radically changed my life. Bill and I had just finished dinner in the parish rectory. "Jim, would you like to be pastor of a larger parish? Bill, would you like if I requested a leave of absence?"

There was an awkward silence. Bill offered me a way to advance. I called for a retreat. What was given as a confirmation of my ministry was taken as if it were a threat. What was that all about? I had no idea nor did Bill. We were both caught by surprise. I told Bill that I had answered him without thinking. We agreed that I should take time to reflect on his offer and my request.

I should have been pleased with his offer. It would put me on the fast track in the promotion pool. I could become a Monsignor, maybe even a Bishop. Bill eventually became a Cardinal. I could be working with and enjoying the companionship of friends in high places: "I coulda been a contender. I coulda been somebody".

Until I unthinkingly uttered these eleven words I had lived as if the will of the Bishop is the will of God. Why else did I not murmur a word of protest about working as a chancery official and a pastor after years of intensive study preparing to be a seminary teacher? Returning from six years of study in Rome I was primed and ready to teach theology in the Seminary where I had studied before being sent abroad. In Rome I had been taught by some of the best teachers in the Catholic Church. Their texts and lectures were in Latin, the precise language of Roman Catholic theology. I learned all that was worth knowing about God, God's people, God's book, God's son, and God's plan of salvation. I learned more about God and Son than one would think is humanly possible. I learned it in the language of scholars, not in the language of chancery officials and surely not in the language of pastors. It was only right and just that I be assigned to teach. But the Bishop had other ideas, other assignments. He put me to work as an administrator. I obeyed him without question and without a murmur. That is how I was raised. Not my will, Your Excellency, but thy will be done. Your will is God's will. Little did I know then that my split-second refusal of a promotion offer would be the death knell of this "will of God" piety.

That death knell began to toll in the following weeks. My reaction to Bill's offer began to feel more and more like an amazing grace – especially when I began to re-read my past parish bulletins. Every one began with a cartoon which featured my main message that Sunday. Reflecting on these bulletins I came to see that accepting a promotion would not be a move in the right direction.

The 12/14/69 bulletin included what I called A Priest's Litany. It was a self-directed alert made public:

From becoming a middle class priest,
From forgetting those who suffer;
From getting stale in my ideals as a priest;
From professionalism, deliver me, Mary.

The 2/15/70 bulletin featured a Charlie Brown cartoon which reminded my parishioners and me about the cut-rate price we look for in helping those in need:

Linus pontificating to Charlie Brown in four frames:
When I get big I'm going to be a humble little country doctor./ I'll live in the city, and every morning I'll get up, climb into my sports car and zoom into the country!/ Then I'll start helping people…I'll heal everyone for miles around./ I'll be the world's famous little country doctor.

The 3/22/70 bulletin included a Charlie Brown cartoon that pointed to how we tend to be the exact opposite of Jesus: where he humbled himself for our sake we tend to humble others for our sake.

Linus: I'm interested in learning how to develop a real concern for others… /Charlie Brown: You mean you want to be concerned about those who are less fortunate than you?/ Linus:

No, I want to be concerned about those who are MORE fortunate than I am./ I want to bring them down to my level.

It is no wonder that after months of prayer and thought I asked for a leave of absence to live and work with the poor. Finally, I had the will to put my will above the bishop's. He knew that my will was a determined will. We already had had a confrontation about my residence. I wanted to identify more with the poor by living in a trailer. But the bishop would not allow it – too undignified. So I converted our kindergarten classroom into an apartment for Bill and me. I was determined to bring the standard of my living quarters down a notch. The apartment was built by the men of the parish at a cost of $9,278.72. (Anything over $10,000 required the permission of the Bishop). Clearly, a bigger parish and a bigger rectory were not the right way to go for me.

But this first step away from hell and the almighty white guy with a beard had its dark side. I moved six nuns into a rectory where two priests had lived. The nuns lost a comfortable and well-deserved home. They worked hard, day in and day out. Parents lost a kindergarten that eased the burden of parenting and gave their children a leg-up on education. No small loss.

Neither nuns nor parents were consulted. In a later edition of parish history my decision was described as an economy move, since the parish had been in financial straits. But it was a decision driven by my desire to identify with the poor. In the end I did nothing that helped the poor. And I messed up the lives of those I should be helping- my teachers and parishioners. I proved the point that being forty years old can be dangerous. That's the age when a mature and settled person can make silly and even devastating decisions. A thinking person's mind can easily turn to mush.

But sometimes even a wrong decision can be an occasion of grace. The move to smaller quarters told me where my heart was. It is no wonder that after much prayer and thought I asked for a leave of absence. The bishop granted me leave to work with "the poorest of the poor, in any territory I found acceptable."

I was now free to move about the country, and beyond.

4. A BETTER ESCAPE ROUTE?-

Saying no to Phil

It was late in the same spring and I had not yet made my escape. I remember well the thirteen words that had me questioning my sudden and dramatic decision about my ministry to the poorest of the poor. That this should happen even before my ministry began was most disturbing. I had not yet left my parish. The date for my leave of absence had not yet been set. I was waiting for my replacement to be appointed by the Bishop. Then on what seemed to be an ordinary day a parishioner asked me what seemed to be an ordinary question:

"Jim, would you like to meet Father Berrigan?
"Neil, you bet I would!"

Until the above thirteen words were spoken my single-minded intent was to find a ministry in which I could be another St. Francis or Mother Theresa. Suddenly I was anxious to talk with Father Berrigan. Why so? I knew enough about him to suspect that he would try to talk me out of my new-found vocation. Father Berrigan was no Mother Theresa. His way of lifting up the lowly was by putting down the mighty. He was not one to mince words: "The poor tell us who we are. The prophets tell us who we could be. So we hide the poor and kill the prophets." I was conflicted. Why out of the blue was I given the opportunity to meet Phil Berrigan?

And it was out of the blue. Neil had been a Josephite priest, as was Father Berrigan. Neil knew Father Berrigan well and if I remember correctly taught him in the Seminary. Neil had left the priesthood and was now a parishioner in my parish. Father Berrigan was now being held for trial in the county jail run by a warden who just so happened to be a neighbor of my friend Neil. It also just so happened that Neil was a very good neighbor to the warden and convinced him to let me visit his high profile prisoner.

I visited Father Berrigan on a regular basis. Phil, as I came to call him, tried to convince me that the best way to help the poor in the United States was to join the anti-Vietnam War movement. He insisted that in matters of war, peace, justice and poverty the leaders of church and state were mostly talk. He did a lot of talking himself in trying to convert me.

I was not a friendly listener. I had been deeply moved by the Vatican Council, referred to by Pope John XXIII as "opening the windows". This Council was the largest and most representative gathering ever held by any church or any other organization. It was the friendliest council in church history. It threatened no one with hell. That was a first. It showed gracious and theological respect for other religions. That was a turnaround. It issued powerfully moving documents on poverty and war, peace and justice. That was most opportune for the 1960's.

I was primed for some remarkable changes in how my church would wage war against war now that the atom bomb was in play. I looked for radical changes in its war against poverty and racism now that our country had declared war on both. Phil tried to convince me that prelates and politicians could talk the talk but not walk the walk. I got a crash course from him on what it takes to stop a war that drafted heavily from the inner cities and depleted heavily public money that could have been used to wage war on the poverty in the same inner cities. Eventually, I might add, Dr. Martin Luther King made the same point.

Phil tried to get me to bite the bullet. His trial was to be held in Harrisburg, Pa. That is where I had worked as a priest for about twelve years. He wanted me to use my good name as a chancery official and pastor to take a public stance against the war. He wanted me to speak to as many groups as possible and so improve his chances for a jury that would be fair.

I resisted the temptation. I said no. I had been given a leave of absence to live and work with the poorest of the poor. My heart was set on doing just that. I had no intention of getting involved in any anti-war movement. I don't know how I resisted Phil's persuasive arguments. I suppose having experienced saying "no" to my Bishop's promotion offer helped in saying no to Berrigan's Peace-movement offer. I would take the escape from the traditional setting of my faith allowed me by my bishop.

Once I began to move about the country in the summer of 1971 , in search of a mission to the poor, I was bewitched, bothered and bewildered by my Church's Pentecost prayer:
"Come Holy Spirit, enkindle in us the fire
 of divine love, and we shall renew
 the face of the earth."

That prayer, inspired by Psalm 104, praises God for seeing to it that planet earth will give us wine to gladden our hearts, food in due season, and will fill us with good things. The psalm proclaims that the Creator is taking care of this personally. But the Pentecost hymn proclaims that God expects us to get the job done. The renewal of the face of the earth clearly is in our hands not in the hands of its creator.

I was bewitched by a prayer that has been chanted down through the centuries. I was bothered and bewildered by the fact that countless images of God sang this Pentecost chant in the pews but not in the streets, and surely not in the ghetto streets. Countless images of God are bewildered by another chant, the one History sings: "Planet earth will never have a new face." No wonder that countless images of God are still scrounging for the crumbs under Lazarus' table. I knew I could not change history. But I could change something. I began by taking a bite out of "The Big Apple."

Manhattan

In those days you could not turn a corner without bumping into "dreamers" like me. On one corner a group would be selling the notion "Dare to be Great!" A block away others

would be preaching love and togetherness with the chant "Spirit
in the flesh". Love and togetherness were being preached on
sidewalks and in the parks. Yes, we were naive but sometimes
it is only the naive who can sniff out the emptiness of the
agenda and the promises of those "in charge."

I wandered into a Pete Seeger Concert in Central Park. He
was singing his version of the Pope's "Peace on Earth". Who
could ask for more? A sign from heaven right there in central
park!

I visited the Little Brothers of the Gospel right off the
Bowery. In approaching their humble abode an elderly and
rather feeble Italian man warned me about how dangerous this
neighborhood was. He insisted on walking with me to protect
me. He walked without fear. Was he carrying a pistol or a
parable in his pocket? Clearly he was happy to protect me.

The Brothers lived in a store front with a slightly Bohemian
look, featuring a loaf of bread and a bottle of wine in the
window and a cardboard sign with a quote from their founder.
Every Brother had a part-time job. One was a janitor for three
apartment buildings. Their mission was largely one of being "a
friendly presence" in the neighborhood.

I would eventually live with a priest in Harrisburg who was a one man mission with the same mission as the Little Brothers of the Gospel. It was so rough where he lived that each time he left he had to put his little TV and guitar in the trunk of the car before driving away. Not once did he resent the fact that his place was often broken into. But his person was never threatened by gun, knife or fist. That would have been a mortal sin in the neighborhood in which he was revered.

One time I was staying there when he was away. During the night I heard the door being kicked in and the search for something to drink. I tried to be quiet but one of them heard me move: "We're coming up. We got a gun." "You better get the f--- out of here. I called the police ten minutes ago." I lied. But they hesitated. They were not sure if I was bluffing. They talked over the pros and cons and finally left. I was afraid to go downstairs even when the police knocked on the door. Of course, the cops told my friend when he returned. He never stopped teasing me about that.

Out West

I spent a week of prayer with The Little Brothers of the Poor in a Detroit slum before heading out West to visit Indian reservations in New Mexico and Arizona.

My first stop was with a priest taking up residence in an abandoned and unpretentious government office building on a Navajo reservation. He was starting a parish there. His right arm was an Indian woman raising four children. She had no husband, and was burdened with a drink problem. But she had the poise and the ability to get people to work.

The Navajos there lived in Hogans, eight-sided wood-mud huts, about 15 to 20 feet in diameter. The one I visited was "middle-class". It had a floor and two beds. Thirteen Navajos lived in a room crammed with Navajo stuff. Everything looked and smelled clean.

I then visited the Hopi Indian mission on the First Mesa, a 500 foot high plateau approachable only by a steep, winding and unnerving road. The inconveniences were not inconsequential. There were no electric lights. Water had to be pumped up and then carried to each home. The tradition is that the Hopi Indians lived on mesas because they wanted a life without war. They valued peace over prosperity.

The children roamed freely and safely despite the lack of any fences. The ancient dances were still danced in this thousand year old village. Missionaries were allowed to come and speak freely – but not allowed to build churches.

Two sad ironies come to mind.

A historical placard in the Chamber of Commerce Museum in Gallup, New Mexico, noted that Coronado and his army, searching for the seven cities of gold, "visited" the Zuni Indians. The word "subdued" would have been more to the point. It took the Spanish less than two hours to just about wipe out the Zunis. What kind of "visit" was that?

I took four Indian children to visit Kit Carson's Cave. On returning back to the village one of the girls told me her friend was afraid to come with us because she might be killed by the Indians. She was an Indian. What kind of education was she getting?

I made no commitments since I planned to go to South America before making any decisions. My parish in Harrisburg had adopted a parish in Chimbote, Peru, after it had been devastated by an earthquake. I knew I would be welcome there.

5. FROM BROOKLYN TO PERU -

A few laughs, a few graces

Two priest friends drove me to Pier III. One of them knew someone high up in the tugboat business. He made arrangements for my passage to South America on a Colombian freighter.

I was all set to board the ship but the Captain would not allow it. He had reserved the one and only passenger cabin for his girl friend. He was not going to give that up for a priest. The Company man was trying to get me on another ship scheduled to sail a week later. I said, "No way!"

I sat my roman collar self in the office of the Ship's Company, surrounded by my luggage. I hung on that cross for about three hours. Longshoremen would come bursting in preceded by exquisite cursing and swearing. Each would get red faced and stutter an apology on seeing the roman collar. (In those days the collar commanded the utmost respect). My presence became a source of entertainment for those working in the office. Word got around to the Italian and Irish hard hats: "Priest dumped on by Captain!" They said "No Way!" They sent out for some ice cream for me and tried to pressure the

Captain to put me in one of the cabins reserved for the crew. But they were powerless. Finally one of the hard hats made a decision: this is a job for Arni.

In came Arni, a soft spoken man in a soft white shirt and dainty cuff links. And yet any fool could see that Arni did not take any crap from anyone. He redid the Captain's certificate to include extra passengers - and extra life preservers. He had the hard hats take my luggage aboard. I got a room and a free box of Fab to do my laundry. What a guy! He could get the big job done and still take care of the small details.

All's well that ends well, especially since the Captain's girl friend spent a lot of her time on deck conversing with me, in front of all the crew – and the captain. Yes indeed, my friends, no doubt about it, The Force was with me.

But then again was it?

The harbor pilot set my nerves on edge trying to convert me to Protestantism while guiding the ship into Baltimore to take on more cargo. He said I could watch him at work. Before I knew it he was saying "Jesus, yes" and "the Pope, no" while supposedly tending to his "starboard lefts" and "starboard rights." I hated to cut into his Jesus enthusiasm but his seeming inattention to piloting was making me nervous. Worse yet, his over-attention to Jesus made me wonder about the dangers of misplaced zeal for Jesus. Was I also off on some kind of a toot?

The second mate put me on the spot when asking me how he should go about teaching religion to his children. He had no confidence in priests and nuns. He intended to instruct them as Voltaire AND Teilhard de Chardin would instruct them. Father La Croce, how would you go about doing this? I stalled, stuttered and stammered. That was the best I could do. Not exactly a confidence builder for one supposedly probing new horizons of faith.

The crew reminded me how easy it is to allow others to pay for your mistakes. At 4:00 a.m., a few days into the voyage, I was awakened by all kinds of shouting. How would you react? Well that's how I reacted. I prayed. Then I panicked. This was followed by a "what the hell" when I looked out of my porthole to see the gangplank being lowered into the ocean.
What an odd way to abandon ship was my first thought. But then I saw another ship heading toward us. As it turned out two

stowaways were found aboard that ship. I found out later they were the stowaways the crew had failed to stow away in Miami as planned and paid for.

The two who were supposed to be the stowaways of the crew were now the prisoners of the crew. What a lesson. It is so easy to allow others to pay for your mistakes.

The dream turned out to be my most reassuring experience. It helped me say "Amen" to my great escape. I had been all pumped up while making my missionary excursion in Manhattan and out West. But on the high seas I began to wonder whether the force was with me. Not so much because of the incidents just noted. I was vulnerable to doubts and fears mostly because I had broken away from long-cherished moorings and was now sailing into the great unknown. The freighter was moving along nicely but I began to feel that I could very well be going upstream without a paddle. My "no" to a bigger parish may have been driven by romantic idealism not by divine inspiration. I had never before put my will above that of the bishop. I had always been a company man. My inclination was not to take risks. What the hell was I thinking?

As this question intensified so did my dreams. One dream was so vivid that it seemed to be more like a vision. Scoff all you want but there are some, like myself, who respect the fact that dreams may be more than dreams when their faith is up for grabs and the chips are down.

Heavy lunches helped account for my very vivid dream. Playing ping-pong helped shape its content.

The heavy lunches were unavoidable. I ate with the crew. I ate like the crew. My plate was heavily laden with three piles - mashed potatoes, spaghetti, and rice- plus a huge piece of chicken. This was served with red wine followed by rich pastries and ice cream. Imagine eating all that then lying down while sailing on a freighter that is rocking gently like a cradle. Vivid dreams came easily and often.

Ping pong was unavoidable. That was about it as far as entertainment was concerned. This was ok by me. My skill at the ping-pong table ingratiated me with the crew. They were delighted with my overhand smash shots, especially when used against several unpopular officers. I also had a drop shot that would fall just over the net. With that shot my opponent could easily be "smote in the groin" (to use a biblical phrase) in lunging to return it. I learned about the drop shot in the seminary. My seminary training was already serving me well. Ping Pong helped me communicate with the crew and, as I am about to explain, helped God communicate with me.

In my dream the old Jim and the new Jim were playing the game called "God speaks". They were going at each other as if in a ping-pong game (no surprise there).

The New Jim: When God speaks the words spoken are barely discernible. It's as if God is a babbling infant or I am hard of hearing. Am I right in thinking God told me to take a leave of absence?
The Old Jim: Idiot! God doesn't speak to the likes of you. He speaks to the bishops and the Pope. The bishop was going to send you to a bigger parish. That was the will of God.

The New Jim: But that means God speaks to us only through guys. How can that be?

The Old Jim: God is a guy himself. Not that he has a "you know what". But God insists on being called "Father" and on always being referred to as "He." The bible and creeds make that perfectly clear. Case closed!

The New Jim: How come God speaks only to guys living along the Mediterranean?

The Old Jim: (getting professorial) "Spiritus spirat ubi vult", that is, The Spirit breathes wherever it chooses to breathe.

The New Jim: The hell you say! You dare to suggest that all who do not live along the Mediterranean are the lesser children of God! Tell me this. How come the Jewish, Christian and Muslim Mediterranean guys to whom God has "spoken" have been at each other's throats down through the ages? What's that all about?

The Old Jim: Sin, sin, sin. Case closed!

The New Jim: What's with this "case closed" business? I've had it with "case closed"! How can any case be closed? If there is one thing that is certain about God it is God's will to be a

silent, unseen, and barely discernible presence on planet earth.
No case is closed. Case closed!

Upon waking up I sat up and said yes, yes, yes. I resolved to
live by my dream. That dream had the force of a vision. It
assured me that inaudible mumblings from God are the most I
can expect.

In trying to make the case that I can rightly refer to my dream
as if it were a vision I remind you of the story of the drowsy
afternoon in which Abraham was promised a son by God
(Genesis, chapter 18). In this story the Lord supposedly
appeared as three men who were served a meal by Abraham, a
meal of choice bread, tender veal, curds and milk.

Could it be that Abraham ate this meal himself and in the heat
of the day snoozed and dreamed that God promised him a son?
His dream would not be like my ping-pong dream because in
those days it was believed that God spoke clearly and forcefully
to the Patriarchs and other special guys. But surely it was a
dream visit not a house visit. If Abraham had really cooked a
meal for three guys Sarah would have noticed. She would not
have reacted as she did to the good news: What, two old coots

having a kid? She probably added, though it is not in the story: What, you doing the cooking?

The story ends on a note familiar to many couples: You laughed said Abraham! I did not said Sarah! Yes you did said Abraham. As you know, Abraham's dream had the ring of truth.

The woman on board was a grace in more ways than one. Other than ping-pong the presence of "the beauty and the priest" was the only entertainment on board. What are they talking about? How can they spend so much time talking? What is going to happen next? Will anything happen?

I was cautious and shy but clearly enjoying our conversations. She was casual and polite but clearly enjoying our conversations. We always met on deck. Neither one made any moves. It was like those romantic comedies when the two never kiss. The fact that we were so careful and correct in our behavior only made this scenario more sensual. We were a veritable soap opera.

I do not mention her name only because I do not recall it. It was clear to both of us we would never meet again.

As the woman and I watched the process of docking at Callao, Peru, I was acutely aware that she, like all women, was stamped with the primitive stories that the Eve was last in creation (Gen. 2:22) and first in Sin (Gen. 3:6) rather than with the much later and more theologically developed story that Adam and Eve were created simultaneously and that both were given dominion over nature (Gen. 1:27-28).

Judaism and Christianity have had women live by the more primitive Genesis stories as long as they could get away with it. Dare I mention also the legend of Lilith, Adam's first wife, banished from Eden for refusing to take the missionary position in sex with Adam – and for being uppity in other ways?

Standing with "the woman" raised in me an unnerving question. Is not South America even more patriarchal and sexist than North America? Hells bells, what was I getting myself into? Maybe I should just visit my adopted parish in Chimbote and head back to the States. It was with that burden on my shoulders that I walked down the gangplank.

Customs was closed when I disembarked. I could not take my luggage with me. I entered Peru with toothbrush, wallet and

passport – divested of all but the basic essentials. How symbolic
could that be?

6. THE PERILS IN PERU -
(Fall 1971 – Winter 1972)

The Good News was the Bad News

Settling in Lima

After a few weeks on shore with the women and men who tended to me and my dream, my doubts and concerns about sexism were soon forgotten. It was not long before I experienced the euphoria that would rightly go with landing on another planet – or in another world. It was as if I had landed in Egypt at the time of Moses. You would think God had only one mission and one mission only - liberation of those enslaved in poverty. You would think that the Gospel meant one thing and one thing only - good News for the wretched masses who say "Help, Help" but little or no news for the pious masses who say "Lord, Lord". You would think that feeding the least was more crucial than saving souls. You would think that the eyes of believers should be on the kingdom on earth as the prize instead of on the kingdom in heaven. You would think that Catholics here were only a cut above the Communists.

Father Joe Nangle, pastor of a middle class parish, was my main man in South America. He was my host, mentor, friend and inspiration. He was a Franciscan priest. He was St. Francis with an attitude. I was not surprised when I picked up his parish bulletin entitled: "Cristo es Revolucion."

Those I was to live with and associate with in South America had only one song in their hearts, the hymn sung in the story of Jesus' pregnant mother: "He will put down the mighty and lift up the lowly." They did not insist that Mary actually sang this song. But this was the text in the birth story that most inspired them. And they rightly revered this song. It became her son's song in his ministry.

Mary's song is a happy tune for all but the mighty. What epic story does not feature the lowly putting down the mighty? Even Hollywood knows the lure of this tale and has made a great deal of money on it. But in the real world putting down the mighty is a risky business, especially if you are unarmed. It can be bad for your health. Ask Jesus, Gandhi, or Martin Luther King. For Jesus, the good news was bad news. Trying to put down the mighty is how Jesus got the reputation of being unarmed but extremely dangerous by the governing powers.

For my new friends in South America, the good news was bad news. They were considered to be unarmed but dangerous by their governments. Phil Berrigan had invited me to be a South American in North America but I had said no. If I said no to Phil why would I say yes to my new friends?

Why stay on these shores?

Why not return to the U.S.?

What was I to do?

I did not want to run because I knew why I wanted to run. I was scared. The theology here was downright scary. Putting down the mighty and lifting up the lowly was taken seriously here. This mission was not for the faint-hearted.

The bishop in charge of a slum area outside Lima, Peru, was in jail for his outspoken speech supporting a workers' movement. One of Peru's most prominent theologians lived in the slums as an example to others. Striking school teachers were in danger of losing more than their jobs. The government here insists on calling all the shots, maintaining the military culture that keeps it in power.

In the spirit of traditional piety, getting my breath so to speak, I visited the room where St. Rose of Lima had her vision of the Christ child. What a shock that was! I was told that while living in this room, a little mud hut at the time, Rose would hang by her hair at prayer in order to stay awake and pray longer.

Now that's a scary story! It is scary mostly because in it the Christ child does not give St. Rose hell for her stupidity: "What kind of a kid do you think I am? Why would you not know that hanging by your hair disgusts me?"

This story is scary also because it suggests that "Christ" does not come to rescue poor benighted souls even when they are hanging by their hair. Such a rescue attempt was made by Jesus the Nazarene over 2000 years ago. Before he could get the job done he was nailed by "the mighty" of the land.

Whether God had closed heaven and the cross was the key that opened it, is not for me to say. I can say that nailing Jesus to it before he could get a head start on his mission gave his followers a helluva job. Jesus' mission to "the mighty" who nailed him became our mission. The cross is not the key to heaven. It is the key to the kingdom of heaven on earth, now in our hands. Eternal rest should be farthest from our minds when we behold the cross. Each time we look at the cross we should roll up our sleeves and punch in the clock for another tough day.

Maybe that's why I said "no thanks" to Phil Berrigan. Maybe the mission to the least must begin with a mission to the mighty. Who wants to take on those who can nail you? Could I do that? Should I do that?

Well I wasn't going to just say "no" to the South Americans, and walk away. I would study the situation and then decide. So it came to pass that in South America I lived the life of a student not that of a man on a mission. But I was an American student. I was a student trained in Rome. Once the emotional dust settled my attitude was "convince me, convert me, give it your best shot".

The Great Debate
Jim vs. the South Americans

South Americans: Look, Jim, the tired, the poor and the huddled masses are miserable mostly because the mighty have a big hand in keeping them so. Sad but true. Most human suffering is caused by bad governance and ungoverned greed. The resources provided freely by our heavenly Father have yet to be shared in a way that would honor our Father's name. Lifting up the lowly cannot be done without putting down the mighty. The two go together like a horse and carriage

Jim: We Catholics in North America have our hands full just trying to stay out of hell. We are in trouble with the Pope about birth control, about divorce and remarriage, about confession before communion and about the ordination of women.

We spend a lot of time trying to fulfill our family obligations, nurture relationships, earning a living and having some free time for fun and games.

History is on our side. No people blessed with prosperity and freedom has been willing to risk that great grace in trying to put an end to poverty and injustice, once and for all. President Franklin D. Roosevelt did take a shot at that grace in 1933. In his "Inauguration Address" he made the charge that the goods of this world were not being distributed fairly: "The rulers of the exchange of mankind's goods have failed." In his "New Deal" he dared to address this injustice by using the government to create jobs and provide social security. The upper class in which he was raised accused him of betraying America's faith in Capitalism. In the capitalist version of the kingdom on earth only business and banks shall create jobs, amass capital, and keep the economy moving. Liberation Theology is not for a nation in which a 1933 Roosevelt was suspect.

South Americans: Look Jim, Roosevelt meant well but his song "Happy Days are here again" was the wrong song. Our song is the one sung by the mother of Jesus while she was pregnant: "He will put down the mighty and lift up the lowly." Roosevelt was a wimp compared to Mary. That is why her song made her son a serious player on planet earth not just one playing around. Most followers of Jesus in North America are just playing around.

Jim: Making war on poverty your way is not a plan we can embrace. We would have to tear down and rebuild all our systems – political, social, and religious. There is no need to do this. Be realistic. We have done quite well in promoting prosperity – better than any other nation.

South Americans: We hope you are not bragging about prosperity built on the backs of Indian Americans, African Americans, and Immigrant Americans. We know you are not bragging about the prosperity paid for by the coal dust in your coal-mining grandfather's lungs. We hope you are not bragging about the wealth amassed before there were unions.

Jim: Yeah, we have our sins like any other nation.

South Americans: Jim, the issue here is not one of sin. Who is without sin? The point is simply this: Jesus and those who carry the cross of his ministry are on a mission from God. Their mission is to see to it that Justice and Peace will finally kiss and make up. They know that Peace without justice is not the peace on earth that is part of the Christmas story. They know that peace without justice is a blasphemy we have yet been unable to avoid. They know that the bomb cannot be the Prince of Peace.

Jim: You've got to be kidding. Come back to earth my friends. Are you trying to tell me Jesus was sent to our planet with an offer we can't refuse: make peace my way or you will have no peace. Make peace my way or the only peace you will ever have is some time off between wars. Was Jesus some kind of Quaker? Were God's last words to Jesus as he was leaving heaven for planet earth right out of The Godfather movie? "Leave the gun, take the cannoli."

South Americans: (laughing) Not bad Jim. Maybe we can use that line. It just about sums up Liberation Theology.

Yes, Jim, the Peace of God came to us wrapped in swaddling clothes, wrapped in poverty, wrapped in the powerless limbs of a new-born infant. Look, the story-teller was saying, God's star led wealthy kings and poor shepherds to get down on their knees and revere those who are too poor and too powerless to help themselves. Bring them gifts. Sing to them. Honor them as if they were his son. Put an end to the brutal heritage of the poor, the wretched, the huddling masses, to the plight of most of humanity – those for whom life is a bitch and then it ends. This is your God speaking. Being marvelous to the least is my son's peace plan. Love, divine style, is the final solution.

Whether or not there were angels singing "Peace on earth" at his birth Jesus of Nazareth went through Galilee like a needle pulling thread, stitching a new life for the poor, the wretched, the huddled masses, working day in and day out with this song in his heart: "Let there be peace on earth and let it begin with me."

If things have not been going so well, you can figure it out for yourself. Two thousand years after the promise of peace in the name of Jesus there is still no peace worthy of the name of Jesus – and you are not even asking, how come?

I had been given plenty to think about. I thought and prayed for weeks on end- along with talking, reading, visiting, taking a crash course on Liberation Theology. The following is my version of its creed and its catechism. It's a damned scary creed and an even scarier catechism:

The Poor Peoples' Creed
Unseemly, Single-minded, Demanding

We believe in

The true presence of Jesus in the least;

The preferential treatment Jesus gave the poor;

The warning Jesus gave about living by the sword;

The prayer of Jesus asking for bread not bombs;

The kingdom on earth as the prize prized by Jesus;

The kingdom on earth as willed by our Father in heaven;

The kingdom on earth as the hallowing of God's name;

The kingdom on earth as the fullest revelation of God.

We know that

Jesus is the revelation of God as an all loving presence, not an all mighty presence. If Jesus had been sent to reveal the presence of God as "The Almighty" then the mighty of planet earth would have been the ones nailed, not Jesus.

Forty years later as I write about this creed an August Wilson play comes to mind, the one in which one of his characters is criticized because "...he done forgot his song, forgot how to sing it. A fellow forget that and he forget who he is."

Last evening I was deeply moved by a scene from the replay of a long-gone T.V. show called "The Rifleman." A dirty, ugly, smelly, and scary bum asks to work for food and board and is hired by The Rifleman. His young son is deeply upset at the thought of living with this bum: "Paw, I can hardly stand to look at him." The father replied: "Neither can I son. That tells us we are worse off than he is."

Questions and Answers

From The Poor People's Catechism

Q. Why has "Liberation Theology" not been featured in Christian theology?

A. From its very beginning Christianity's sacred stories, creeds, and clergy favored and featured "Salvation Theology". No wonder. It is much easier to promote belief in a God whose presence saves us from hell and helps us get to heaven than in a God who is calling us to reshape the face of the earth.

Few dare to believe that God is calling them to help pacify and justly govern our planet by way of creative nonviolence rather than by relying on violence. It was only by a flash flood of grace that liberation theology made its mark in South America.

Q. How was Liberation Theology able to have some success in South America?

A. It highlighted the fact that Christianity has never forged the political will to do what has to be done to renew the face of the earth. The clergy were urged to maintain an ongoing analysis of the social realities but without prejudice to their roles as pastors. Small base communities were formed to educate and encourage the laity as agents of change. The leaders were determined to make it perfectly clear that this was truly a revolution that would put those in power out of power, and that evangelical non-violence was their method of getting this done.

Q. What is it that is most radical about liberation theology?

A. The demand that the poor be the first to suck on the teat of mother church. This meant more than having poor boxes in the rear of the church, having collections for the poor, urging the faithful to be generous to the poor.

The church as an institution must serve the poor, not just individuals or groups within the institution of the Church.

Some theologians even insisted that the Church as an institution should set itself up only among the "least of the brothers and sisters." The middle and upper classes should worship, build schools and build community only among the poor, on real estate occupied by the poor. Why so? Jesus made it perfectly clear that the best place to find him is in the least. Setting up all their parishes among the poor would give Christians their best shot at treating the least as if the least were Jesus.

By "the least" was meant the ignorant, unkempt, and low life wretches believed to be incapable of the virtues cherished by the kempt, the educated and those living the middle and high life.

Q. What is the energy that drove this radical approach to theology?

A. In South America many had had enough with pleas, politics and prayers as the path to a peace with justice.

It was time to put pressure on the mighty by putting them down while lifting up the lowly.

It was time to put an end to our image of God as the Almighty: Enough with believing in God as if we were children; enough with believing in a God who relies on our fear of hell and our lust for heaven. It is time to believe in ourselves. Come loving Spirit and help us renew the face of your magnificent incarnation – planet earth.

Q. What are the chances that liberation theology will flourish? A. From pitiful to none. As you can well imagine, my friends in South America and those who would be my friends in North America were doomed to fail. "The least" with whom Jesus identified do not look like, act like, or smell like Jesus. Once roused to anger they will grab a gun just as quickly as we do.

Almost everyone since day one assumes there will always be wars and rumors of wars. Poverty has always been treated as a managerial problem to be dealt with by politics and economics rather than as a Jesus-driven responsibility of our faith. There has never been a war on poverty like the war Jesus waged. It has always been assumed that such a war cannot be waged, let alone won. There will always be the rich and the poor, the mighty and the lowly. There will never be a kingdom of God on earth. Not even God, those who believe in God, or those who do not, can make this happen.

This sad and sorry assumption was best stated by Immanuel Kant: "Out of the crooked tree of humanity no straight thing can ever be made."

Q. What are the chances that Communism will provide a better life for "the least"?

A. A woman in a novel by Pearl Buck complains about the Chinese Communist attempt to straighten out humanity: "We are now ruled by the children of peasants. Heaven and earth are upside down. Those who were high are made low – or dead. Those who were low are raised up and they rule. We must wait a hundred years, until the times are set right again." The woman did not believe a state could make agriculture, industry and commerce serve the poor and punish the rich. Later in meeting an old man more bitter than herself she said: "At least the rich are not so rich and the poor are not so poor." He responded: "Give us time, and some will be rich again and some will be poor again. It is man's fate."

Q. What is the Christian way out of this sorry mess?

A. Heaven is the only way out of this sorry mess. This sorry mess is why we have heaven. On planet heaven God will make all things right.

Surely the Nazarene did not expect us to identify with the least as thoroughly as he did.

Surely he did not mean that those who do not do so will go straight to hell – not even allowing for any "excuse me; I did not know it was you".

Surely, peace on earth can only be a cleaned up version of the peace of Caesar. Surely, the prosperity that comes with the promise of peace must be nothing more than a cleaned up version of Capitalism.

Q. Why is this not the best possible answer? Why is it not even a good answer?

A. This "solution" takes the steam out of our ministry to the poor. It can even be said that it makes heaven the greatest enemy of the poor. It sounds silly I know but it really is so.

Counting on heaven belittles the plight of the "the least" – and, yes, even the ministry of Jesus to them.

Chimbote

I finally made my way to the parish my parish had adopted. I got there by a "Collectivo"- a taxi shared by others. For long distance traveling you must wait until the car is filled before you can go. It is a cheap but dangerous way to travel, as full speed ahead means more trips, more money. The roadside latrines are nothing to write home about or, something to write home about. Talking was minimal. We were cheek by jowl, but not with the same cheeks and jowls. It did not take long to grow weary driving five hours in such close and uncomfortable quarters.

The bishop's house was like a little doll house – neat and delicately furnished. It did not belong on the slim coastline of Peru roughened out with mountains and jungle. The bishop himself seemed ill-fitted for Chimbote, a rough wide open city of about 200,000, up from 5,000 twenty years earlier. The city had "potential" muscle for Peru with its fishing and steel industries, citizens who were relatively non-traditional because they came from other areas, and, above all, a clergy that was open to change.

   But the bishop had no leadership ability. Even in his own house he leaned heavily on his servants. At least he was kind and down to earth and let others go ahead and do whatever they do.

   And the city was rife with problems. The prison, the institution that best reflects the soul of a society, was unbelievably abominable. The Chimbote hospital had about 60 beds for its 200,000 people. The bed sheets were boiled in large tin cans. Clinics were available for those who could pay the price. About 40% of the people were unemployed. About 40 slum areas made up the bulk of the population.

   Chimbote was basically a big slum. The upper level slums were for those working. The lower level slums for those not working. About 6,000 worked in the fishing industry and about 25,000 in the steel industry. And there's the rub.

The fish was converted into fishmeal, food for cats in the U.S. – not to provide a highly nutritious diet to the citizens of Peru. Money provided by North American generosity went mostly to projects like building roads to a copper mine run by or benefiting American capital.

A priest I befriended gave me a tour of the Star-Kist Tuna plant in the Santa Valley. About 150 men hauled the fish from the boat to a plant where about 400 women skinned and cleaned the fish. There used to be 700 Star-Kist male employees but most jobs were contracted out once they demanded social security. The women went on strike several years before I arrived. Star-Kist then moved its canning process to Puerto Rico. But the government said, no canning plant, no fishing. Star-Kist returned. In my diary I have no notes about the outcome of that sad story.

You may recall that my parish adopted this parish after it was hit by an earthquake. The front wall of the church was completely destroyed and had not been replaced. At Sunday Mass the church was filled with sunshine and breezes. Birds, dogs and children roamed freely. Informality was the keynote. One woman went up to the celebrant during mass to ask him something. Why wait? After Mass a proposed change in the hours of mass was put to a voice vote.

Whether liberation theology can ever lead the Chimbotes of this world out of such a sorry mess is not for me to say. I do know that we who believe in God and Son are more accustomed to revere them for their power to save us than for the power given us to save a Chimbote, wherever it may be.

We love our traditional stories of divine power that promises heaven and threatens hell. And yet, you must admit that the power of God sending people to heaven or hell is divine child's play compared to the power of God using the likes of us to usher in the divine kingdom on earth. That is the power of a God truly worthy of the name of God.

What's the lesson here? Surely Jesus does not expect us to lift up the lowly by putting down the mighty? He may as well ask us to be suicide bombers in his name. Mary can sing all she wants about her magnificent son. We are ordinary people.

Maybe so. But if so, we should stop talking as if we were images of God, reborn in Christ, temples of the Holy Spirit, followers of Jesus etc., etc., etc. How can we not walk the walk that goes with such talk? When a lawyer asked Jesus what he had to do to be his follower Jesus told him to sell what he had, give it to the poor, and then he could walk with Jesus.

Don't panic my friends. That text should be read as a lesson being taught to that man on that day in that place. That's the only way Jesus ever taught. He was not a philosopher or a theologian. His words were not for publication. They were seeds to be sown.

But there is a lesson here for us in Jesus' words to the lawyer, even though we cannot take them literally. They tell us where the heart of Jesus was. That's how you tell where a person's heart is – when they exaggerate. When they demand the impossible it is their heart speaking. Once you know where Jesus' heart is you know in what direction he is pushing you. You then should be more open in pushing yourself in that direction.

Even a small symbolic act would be a good start.

You may not want to applaud the U.S. Marine who distributed ten coins at a checkpoint in Iraq. One side asked: "Where will you spend eternity?" The answer was given on the other side, stamped with John 3:16. The marine was telling them that all Muslims are going straight to hell.

You may want to pay to put up a Luke 4:18 sign everywhere you see one citing John 3:16. You may want to sit behind the goal posts at a televised football game holding up a Luke 4:18 sign so it will show up on the TV when the extra points are kicked. I am sick and tired of seeing only John 3:16 signs along the highway and on TV.

On horseback in the High Sierras

Father Jack, Smiling Jack to me, took me with him to the Church of Santiago (St. James). The first ninety miles into the mountains was by jeep. The road was so narrow that on a day assigned to downhill traffic an uphill vehicle had to back up, day or night, until it came to a place in the road that would allow the downhill car, truck or bus to get by. The rest of the trip was by horseback.

I was to lead the way since I was riding the mother of Jack's very fidgety horse. Jack was the first stranger to ride him. Some parts of the road were about five feet wide, mountain wall on one side and a 500 foot drop on the other. You already know that I am a wimp. Smiling Jack could see that I was scared. Only God knows if he had set me up.

Don't worry, Jim, your horse doesn't want to fall any more than you do, and is sure footed… slight pause… unless stung by a bee or road workers start dynamiting.

Jack's "unless" came to pass. A road crew began blasting away. Jack's horse skittered. We had to stay on the horses since there was no room to dismount. I said what bad luck. Does this nag have a reverse? Smiling Jack said what good luck. There will probably be no more blasts. We can move on safely. As we rounded the bend we saw the path was just about covered by gravel from the dynamiting done somewhere above us. Ahead of us were a man, woman and some cattle. What good luck said Jack. We'll see if they can make it over the gravel pile. They did. We now had some room to dismount. We did so and walked through the rubble.

Jack told me that this was not the road he considered most dangerous. There were roads to two other villages that made even him nervous. What good luck I said, not trying to hide the sarcasm and already thinking about the return trip.

On arriving we were met by the villagers walking behind a band, leading us to the Church. This was not a grand salute to our arrival. The band had been hired by the family of a woman who had died six months ago. This was a funeral procession.

Without comment we duly took our places in the procession to the church, behind someone carrying a photograph and the sombrero of the dead woman. After mass we processed to the cemetery where a group of women were seated around the gravesite, solemn faced, tuning into the spirit world while waiting for the body. Smile if you will but I did not do so. I was deeply moved. Maybe I was just tired and on edge from the trip. Maybe something wonderful was going on at that gravesite.

After Jack did what priests do at gravesites the band led the villagers to a pavilion where free food and drink were provided by the family of the deceased – as is the custom on planet earth.

Eventually Smiling Jack and I retired to his modest quarters so that we could share our experiences in English and share a shot or two of Jack Daniels.

What followed was the strangest damn conversation you ever heard about death and resurrection – topics on the tip of our minds, having just made a dangerous journey and soon to do it over again.

It began with an old joke I had heard about Oral Roberts. Pastor Roberts was having a tomb built for himself in the Holy Land, damn the expense. When he saw the plans for it he was very pleased. That should do very well. But how much will the tomb cost? Two million dollars said his aide. No way said Roberts. That's too much money for just three days use.

Jack: Wrong! Pastor Roberts would get more than his money's worth. He and his body will be in that tomb until the general resurrection at the end of history. Pastor Roberts is no Jesus. Only Jesus gets to get out the tomb in three days.

Jim: Hold on! I was taught that if I am good I will go to heaven nanoseconds or so after death, after having been cleared by "the Judge". No three days in the tomb and a forty day wait to get into heaven. I was raised to believe that I get a better deal than Jesus.

Jack: Nobody gets a better deal than Jesus. No one gets out of the tomb in less time than Jesus. No one makes it to heaven in less time than he did. You and I will rise up along with everyone else at the general resurrection, as preached by Jesus – and as testified by the ancient tombstones in New England: "Asleep in the Lord".

Jim: Easy on the Jack Daniels, Jack. Or maybe I have had a bit too much. Are you saying that I have no soul, that when my body dies I die?

Jack: Not me, but Ezekiel and Jesus. Ezekiel prophesies that God will put flesh on the dry bones of the righteous of Israel, not on their souls. Jesus preached resurrection of the body not immortality of the soul. Jesus was no Plato. And like Ezekiel he preached communal not personal resurrection. Note well: Resurrection is not the icing on the cake of immortality. Resurrection is the cake.

Jim: O.K. Now I have a question for you: Is it possible that there will be no resurrection cake for anyone until the poor, the wretched and the huddled masses are eating cake on planet earth?

Jack: Definitely! That is why Jesus told the parable about inviting the poor, the cripples, the lame and the blind rather than friends and family to our banquets. That is why he tried to scare the Bejesus out of us with his last parable about sending straight to hell anyone who does not treat the least as if they were Jesus.

Jim: Is it possible that those who work for peace and justice on earth are doing more toward getting all of us into heaven than all the other followers of Jesus?

Jack: Indeed it is. There will be no kingdom of heaven for anyone until there is a kingdom on earth for everyone.

Jim: I hear you. But I am no happier than my friends and family in thinking about the possibility that the resurrection is delayed until all this kingdom business is sorted out. Whenever I discuss my mom's funeral I have her going straight to heaven, not into a Big Sleep.

Jack: Poor Jim! Unhappy about a delayed resurrection. How unhappy is Jesus knowing that so few of us work our butts off for the "the least"? Does he settle for a reasonable facsimile? How could he do that in light of his last parable about sending most of us to hell?

Jim: I expect the last judgment parable is more a kick in the butt than an actual threat. I expect that liberation theology is the same kind of kick in the butt.

Jack: I don't doubt his hell-threatening parable is a kick in the butt. It tells us that God and Son will not give up on their mission to establish a kingdom on earth. And obviously they are not going to get the job done as described in the last book of the bible. Such apocalyptic blood-letting would be a sorry solution for two lovers whose love knows no bounds.

With that, my friends, I close my story about Jack, Jack Daniels, and me in the High Sierras.

Farewell to South America

In the matter of peace and justice on earth we are the prisoners of our history and our religious traditions. And I do mean "we". My noble thoughts are for the most part only the conjectures of a guilty bystander. I have no cause to take the 'high ground' in sharing my experiences. I will say that as often as I can.

Before I take leave of my hectic and sometimes harrowing accounts of what faith in God seems to demand when the poor get poorer, the rich get richer, and hate and greed show their staying power, I want to share a few fond memories of my experiences in South America.

I remember helping American missionary priests hide caches of canned food and dry goods for workers preparing for a long strike. I praised one priest for his leadership role. I still remember his reply: "Jim, when the hammer drops my bosses will bring me back to the States. These people will take the blows." The few times I have told that story tears always come, tears of joy for having worked with such people.

I remember flying into the jungle with a photographer from *National Geographic* and a linguistics expert. The anthropologist friend who set this up did so reluctantly. He did not trust linguistics experts. He heard that in Vietnam they helped the U.S. government rather than the natives. He did not even trust my hope of working with these people as a missionary priest. I would never get to know them he told me. You will not even learn their names. These are kept secret because the evil spirit has power over those whose names are known. When friends meet, one friend will say "Is it you?" The other will answer "It is I."

As it turned out, I left the jungle to join the anti-Vietnam war movement in the States. I left the jungle but the jungle did not leave me. I was deeply touched by the practice of religion there. It was a fearsome place and yet it favored a fearless relationship to God and one without the need to stand on ceremonies. The spirit world was accepted without question and one's place in it was not connected to how one behaved.

Their reliance on "visions" and their lack of fear of God touched me deeply, as you will notice in reading this book. I thank them for that.

I spent my forty-second birthday swimming in that jungle river in my birthday suit. This was a long way from the banks of the Susquehanna River where I had lived and worked as a chancery official and pastor. It was not the Jordan River. I heard no voice from heaven saying that I was a beloved Son of God and that God was pleased with me.

But I was not without grace. A few days after my birthday swim a rich and well placed man, swimming in his private pool, said to me: "I envy you, your youth, your ideals and what you are setting out to do."

I was preparing to meet Ernesto Cardenal, a contemplative priest who, at the moment, was moving about beneath the radar screen of his government. He was considered unarmed but dangerous. He later became a key figure in a revolutionary war. I was to deliver Gustavo Gutierrez's book on liberation theology along with a personal note from Gutierrez. I was told that the last person who tried to visit Ernesto Cardenal had been questioned for eight hours as to the purpose of his visit. My friends suggested I look as "touristy" as possible. They insisted I wear the roman collar and gave me Indian arrows and baby dolls to carry. This gave the border guards a laugh. I chuckled my way into Nicaragua eager to meet with Ernesto Cardenal.

I visited a coffee shop for three days waiting for a meeting to be set up. Meanwhile, I read the book on Liberation Theology. In doing so I had the feeling that Gustavo Gutierrez was peeking into my soul as well as his own. What a joy to see my soul in his book. Finally a Dutch priest with an eye patch picked me up and drove me to Cardenal's family home. They made me feel at home. Ernesto trapped me into siding with him in a playful argument with his somewhat traditional mother about the value of Lenten rules. She was no pushover. She said that his best poem was "A Prayer for Marilyn Monroe." That brought a laugh. Ernesto Cardenal was the poet laureate of the liberation movement. I will always remember that moment between Ernesto and his mother. Their intimacy was not tempered by the fame and fury that went with his job.

Yes, my friends, the graces I was experiencing in South America were more than I could ever have hoped for. The lessons learned and the questions asked gave me a new lease on my life of faith. But it was these very graces that brought me back to the States.

Former parishioners were being arrested for acts of civil disobedience against the Vietnam War. I felt guilty because I helped to get them to the point where they might end up in jail. I was not with them when they needed me the most. I could no longer remain on the sidelines. I would accept the offer made by Father Berrigan. I would try to learn how to put my body where my heart was. I would learn to do this with my friends in the United States of America.

7. BACK IN THE STATES - (Winter 1972 – Spring 1977)

My trustworthy friends

I returned to Harrisburg, Pa. all fired up about peace and justice. After a brief visit with my family I lived and worked with those who waged an unofficial, unsupervised and sometimes unlawful war against the war in Vietnam. This required a lot of traveling. I drove so many used cars that a priest friend with whom I lived in the ghetto told me his neighbor thought I was dealing in stolen cars. He wanted in on the deal. Many times other cars passed me on the highway and I heard the drivers shouting, get that piece of s--- off the road. I was meeting and working with anti-war activists in Harrisburg, Baltimore and Manhattan.

In Harrisburg I was warmly welcomed by the anti-war activists. They needed all the help they could get. Many jobs in the city and environs were government or military jobs. Central Pennsylvania was not friendly to Catholics. When I was in the Bishops' office one of our priests had to pose as a business man buying land for an ice cream plant so that we could buy land for a new parish. Now I was with Phil Berrigan, a catholic priest charged with conspiracy against the government. Defending Phil was more difficult than buying land for a Church. He needed all the help he could get. I began spending my good name on a Catholic priest who was considered dangerous to and by the government. It took a lot of spending, almost more than I had to give.

Meanwhile, Jane Fonda had no luck in finding a venue in Harrisburg to present her slide show on Vietnam. The anti-war "Headquarters" asked me to call her. I put off doing so. I was ambivalent. I was too busy working for Phil. Finally she called me. She convinced me to do what I could. I did find some places for her. I never regretted it. She was down to earth and did everything she was told to do. Button up one more button, Jane, this is Harrisburg not Hollywood. She carried her own equipment. She was also very friendly and down to earth. Sometimes too down to earth as when she asked me to buy some tampons for her.

And she had a sense of humor. That came out one evening while acting as her "bodyguard" – my priesthood as her protection. As I was escorting her to the podium one of my former female parishioners jumped on me knocking me to the floor, calling me a dirty communist. Later Jane told me with that famous Fonda smile on her face: "I have toured this country from sea to shining sea and this is the first time my bodyguard was attacked."

I was involved in many meetings in Manhattan, Harrisburg and Baltimore. We were planning for Phil's release from prison and the establishment of "Jonah House" in Baltimore. It would house activists who would promote civil disobedience.

It was in Manhattan, in walking those mean streets, that I began developing an attitude. In Levis, T-shirt, unshaven and a cigarette dangling from my lips even the muggers crossed the street when they saw me coming. I now had "the look". I kid you not. Such is the power of anger wrapped in idealism. Knowing what a wimp I am by temperament you could not have imagined such a change.

The Manhattan meetings are only a blur. We always sat in a circle and almost always on the floor, never knowing who might be sitting next to you – a leggy dancer from the theater, a woman training for the opera, a Jewish atheist (whom I convinced to pray to St. Anthony for finding a parking space). At these meetings I was treated kindly and even with respect, though I was laughed at many times because of my naive comments. Even though I had been to South America I still slipped into old habits of thought. In many ways I was still a boy priest. I was like a fish out of water. Those I lived and worked with were way ahead of me. I could not match their stamina, their humor under fire, their reckless determination, their fierce single-mindedness – all those things so often and so wrongly criticized, some times even by me. Despite the free and easy attitude about sex no one ever tried to tempt me in that regard. Thank God for that because I was very vulnerable.

These were the best of friends. I say this because they talked the talk and walked the walk of the Jesus who lived with, worked with the least and took risks when risks had to be taken. They convinced me that the only way to lift up the lowly at this time and in this place was to put down the mighty. I learned a lot in South America but learning is not the same as risking the fate of lawbreakers, of risking the fate of jailbird Jesus.

In South America I was foot loose and fancy free. The risks were minimal. What I gave was nothing compared to what was given to me. I gorged myself on the goodness of others and gave back only an encouraging word. At best I shared and applauded the anger of the oppressed. My graces were as one dreams grace should be. I went from one up to an upper up. There were no downs. In South America my anger was more a romantic grace rather than a rough and risky grace.

But back in the States grace was its usual edgy self. My bishop, my fellow priests, my former parishioners, most of my friends, and my family did not warmly welcome home the new Jim. Quiet Jim was now loud mouthed Jim. Obedient Jim was disobedient Jim. Well-tempered Jim was angry Jim. The Jim who courted the good will of others, even needed it badly, courted it no longer. The Jim who discussed the defects of tradition calmly and in keeping with the sentiments of the moral majority was no more.

My mom was very upset. I had been her boy the priest. I studied in Rome. I lived and worked with the Bishop. When I came to visit her I drove the Bishop's Oldsmobile 98. I would tell her stories about my life with the bishop. I would tease her about how I teased the Bishop. At school functions I would take his chair on stage instead of mine and the little girl with flowers for the bishop would give them to me instead. Once while the bishop was addressing high school students I fell asleep on the stage, in clear view of all. The bishop tried to embarrass me by announcing "Father La Croce would like to say a few words". I stood up, stammered a bit and then said "I too give you a free day from school." Now instead of living, laughing and working with the bishop he was denouncing me as a Judas.

My mother thought I was having a nervous breakdown. I understood the pain and sorrow that led her to believe this. It was only right that she should feel this way. She was a mother. Someone told me that she was at one of my trials with a purse full of money, ready to pay a fine or bail me out. How agonizing can that be for the mother of a priest?

I felt like a stranger at my former parish, even when talking to the children in the parish school, even while visiting those working in the parish office. Some parishioners believed I was possessed. They asked if they could perform an exorcism on me. I told them to give it their best shot (I can be flippant) and they did.

Others in my parish felt betrayed. I was leaving them, they thought, to do for the poor what I had been doing for them as another Christ. I washed Adam's sin from the souls of their children, forgave their sins, re-enacted the death of Christ at

Mass, fed them the body of Christ, preached the gospel, joined them in marriage, anointed them when sick and buried their dead.

It was only natural that most were shocked when instead of serving the poor as if I were another Christ I went traipsing around the country as if I were another Jesus – lifting up the lowly by trying to put down the mighty and trying to take away the sword of their president. Could you blame them for not giving me a "way to go" Father La Croce? I cannot.

I was not even giving myself a "way to go Jim". I had been ever so happy as a pastor, as evidenced by a gift given to me by a close priest friend. It was a Seth Thomas clock. On the face was engraved this sentiment: "Life began 9:30 a.m., Sept.10, 1965." I don't remember why the inscription said 9:30 a.m. I was never a late sleeper. But I do know why it said September 10, 1965. That was the day I was born again. I was no longer a chancery official. I was now a pastor. I was now able to live as "another Christ" – taking away the sins of a people, feeding them with the bread of life, preaching the good news of salvation.

It was only natural then that I had my doubts about trying to be another Jesus. Jesus lived in an occupied land. I lived in a democracy. Jesus was a Torah Jew. I was a Roman Catholic. Jesus was a rejected prophet. I was a highly respected clergyman. Jesus was highly suspect by those in authority. I was highly favored by those in authority. Jesus was crucified by Rome. I was ordained a priest in Rome. Simply put, I was ordained to be another Christ, not another Jesus.

I was ever so close to washing liberation theology out of my mind, heart and soul. Even given my time in South America a guy like me should never even have been tempted to be an angry agent of radical change in the States. But I was! And for giving into that temptation I have to thank my trustworthy friends. Without them I woulda been an angry wimp. With the greatest reverence and affection I remember them as the monk with an attitude and the marvelous maniacs.

My monk with an attitude

Father Thomas Merton became famous as a convert from a mixed-up fast-paced unbelieving life to a contemplative life bordered with monastic silence. Then he became infamous for his bad-ass attitude about war. I will explain that shortly.

But for the moment let me say that Merton lived the gospel cited in Matthew 26: 52: "Then Jesus said to him, 'Put your sword back into its place; for all who take the sword will perish by the sword'."

You are probably aware of the custom of taking a biblical text and then running with it as far as you can without being mugged for abusing the text. Catholics do this with Matthew 16: 18-19 (about Peter as the rock on which Jesus built his church). Evangelical Protestants do this with John 3:16 (about salvation only for those who believe in Jesus). My monk did this with Matthew 26:52 (about the sword that kills those whose lives it saves).

Jesus' words about putting away the sword were said in one of the more dramatic moments of the Gospel story. It was a dark and dangerous night. Something terrible was afoot. Everyone in Jerusalem was on edge.

Pilate was on edge. The people had welcomed Jesus to Jerusalem singing "Hosanna to the Son of David." That sounded like insurrection to Pilate. Passover week was no time to be fooling around with insurrectionists.

Many of the people who sang "Hosanna" were on edge when Jesus stopped Temple sacrifices. That sounded like blasphemy to them. Had he lost his faith? The sacrifices Jesus stopped were the sacrifices his parents offered to God for him in this very Temple.

Those who loved Jesus' parables were stunned by his parable of the judgment of the nations. It threatened them with hell for not treating the wretched as if they were Jesus. This sounded like lunacy.

No one was singing hosannas by the time the mob mobbed Jesus in the olive garden.

Worse yet, Jesus' hand-picked leaders were making him look like a loser. Judas was about to betray him. His "A" team could not even pray with him. Peter would soon deny him. Even Jesus was falling apart. He did not want to die. He would accept death only if ordered by the will of his Father. Death at this time made no sense to him. The least needed him. His mission was far from completed. It would be a disaster if he were taken down now. He was the best hope peace and the poor ever had. His ministry would be nailed to the cross with his body. It would die with him. It would become the greatest of vanishing acts. He could see his road ministry disappear. He could see our rituals replacing it. It is no surprise to me that two Gospels cite his last words as: "My God, my God, why have you forsaken me?"

Yes, my friends, on that dark and dangerous night the stakes were high and the chips were down. If there ever was a night for sword play this was it. And yet, when a follower cut off the ear of one of the slaves of the High Priest, Jesus said: "Put your sword back into its place; for all who take the sword will perish by the sword."

Well, my monk reasoned, if defending Jesus and his mission does not justify using weapons when is the use of weapons justified? When does defending a country justify war? I must tell you that my monk was not in the best of moods when he asked these questions. He had not gotten over our use of the Atom bomb against Japan. He knew that it hastened the end of the war and so saved many lives. But he was ticked off that some of those involved in its preparation and delivery light-heartedly called it "Fat Boy". He was appalled that we as a people had introduced this terrible weapon of mass destruction. He believed it did not bode well for the soul of our nation. Its soul was now heavily burdened with a peace plan that became known as MAD (Mutually Assured Destruction): If you atheistic commies send your bombs our way we God-fearing leaders of the free world will send ours your way before yours can stop us from destroying you. For this MAD "Godly-Commie Peace Plan" to work our nation had to sustain the will to abort the lives of millions in an apocalyptic instant. This bomb had already been the mother of all abortions in giving birth to countless unplanned and unwanted abortions in a Hiroshima and Nagasaki minute. This bomb was nothing like the Angels' song bursting in air over Bethlehem. This bomb was the Anti-Christmas.

It was in that context my monk developed his attitude about war. I tried my best to run with my monk as far and as fast as I could. It was not easy. As you can see he had the most unrelenting bad-ass attitude anyone could possibly have about waging war in the nuclear age.

But don't worry my fellow Americans. There is an escape clause in what Jesus said about putting away the sword. It came in the following two sentences:

"Do you not think that I cannot appeal to my Father, and he will at once send me more than twelve legions of angels? But then how would the scriptures be fulfilled, which say it must happen this way?"

The army of angels was not used by Jesus in the olive garden only because, in this story, Jesus was destined to die the bloody death predicted by Scripture. Mt. 26:52 is not an anti-war text. On the contrary the reference to God's twelve legions in the very next sentence reminds us of the prevailing biblical image of God as "War Lord". And that, my friends, is one powerful image. Let me tell you about that image as briefly as I can.

Legend has it that God went straight to war against Satan and "his fellow" rebels. God and angels, though pure spirits, are referred to as males. God made no attempt to negotiate, or to rely on infinite love in winning these rebels over. The legend-makers believed that God handles "his" problems pretty much like we do.

Our Bible stories reflect this belief. They tell us that for God war is the solution to all major problems. In these stories God's wars on planet earth began and will end with weapons of mass destruction, water in the beginning and fire at the end. God's most notable wars are linked to his promise to give his people a land of milk and honey. The problem with God's promise was that the land promised was already occupied. God's promise was wrapped in a war.

In his book "What on earth is God doing?" Reynald E. Showers explained that God commanded the Israelites to kill all the inhabitants of the Promised Land so that they would not be tempted to worship their false gods. "In other words, the coming of the Redeemer (through an unsullied Israel) was more essential for the benefit of mankind than the continued existence of the depraved people of Canaan."

There is no war in the Holy Land without God supposedly having a hand in it. Today the holy land is more unholy than holy. In the last book of the bible we read that God will wipe out all sinners in a way that would put any tyrant to shame, and would make Jesus turn over in his grave – if that were possible.

A war that began before the beginning of the world and will end only at the end of the world is a very long war. And you know what happens in long wars. Before you know it you cannot tell the good guys from the bad guys.

"War is us" could very well be the song sung by God and Satan. "Our Father is at war and so are we" could very well be the only song Jews, Catholics, Protestants and Muslims can sing in unison. Both songs provide an ominous soundtrack for the inhabitants of planet earth.

As you can see, defending God as "War Lord" blasphemes rather than glorifies God. I would not go there if I were you.

My monk, with good reason, was totally relentless in trying to bury the image of God and War. He could not do this without an attitude. He was facing some heavy hitters. The bible, the Qur'an, and the traditions of three great religions put God and War together like a horse and carriage. My monk needed attitude. He had attitude. On one occasion he characterized the hierarchy as "jackassing around". This may sound haughty and mean-spirited to you but it is no more so than Jesus characterizing the Pharisees as "whited sepulchers." Both Jesus and Merton had attitude, God bless them.

In the 1960's and 70's Vatican II and Vietnam were twin tornadoes uprooting old ways of thinking about God and War, and about piety and patriotism. But my marvelous monk was a tornado unto himself. He uprooted the images of God held sacred from Day One. In a Merton minute planet earth as God's proving ground became God's playground:

"The Lord made His world not in order to judge it, not in order merely to dominate it, to make it obey the dictates of an inscrutable and all-powerful will, not in order to find pleasure or displeasure in the way it worked: such was not the reason for creation either of the world or of man.

The Lord made the world and made man in order that He himself might descend into the world, that He himself might become Man. When He regarded the world He was about to make He saw His wisdom, as a man-child, 'playing in the world, playing before Him at all times.' And he reflected, 'my delights are to be with the children of men.'"

No, no, no, no you may say. No monk in his right mind should speak of God as creating planet earth as a playground. His son was not sent here to play but to pay for our sins. We are here not to play but to prove ourselves worthy of getting into heaven. God made planet earth as a proving ground. We are but puny and wishy-washy pawns, constantly changing sides in the cosmic war between God and Satan. Planet earth as playground will never replace planet earth as battleground.

So you say! Why then does our story of God begin with planet earth as a paradise, a playground? Why does the story of the son feature him working his butt off to make his part of the planet more and more like a place to play, more like the garden of paradise?

If the ministry of Jesus means anything, my monk had a point. In his life on the road Jesus was not the revelation of God as War Lord but God as Real Estate Lord: "Build a paradise here and then I will come."

If Jesus was the incarnation of God as War Lord he would have been a battlefield kind of guy. He would have led armies. He would never have left home without his sword. He would have struck some mighty blows. Jesus was no such incarnation. In resisting Satan there was not even sword-play. He simply told Satan to get lost, and that was that.

If the hundred or so bible references to the kingdom of God on earth mean anything they suggest that Jesus was sent precisely to make planet earth the best damned playground ever imagined, and to do it with bread not swords. And, as the story goes, partying was part of his master plan. In the story in which Matthew is called to be a follower, Jesus makes it clear that he is a physician who plans to heal the sick (read sinners) by eating and drinking with them (read partying) rather than by denouncing them (see Mk. 2:13-17; Mt. 9:9-13; Lk. 5:27-32)

Little did Jesus and Merton know that in 2008 they would get a "thumbs up" from Stuart Brown, President of the National Institute of Play: "If you look at what produces learning and memory and well being, play is as fundamental as any aspect of life …"

My monk with an attitude needs to be taken seriously. He knew that wherever and whenever the guns start blazing the playground becomes a battleground. He knew that fighting one another and Mother Nature is making us an endangered species. We have been good at making war and pursuing prosperity but lousy at making peace and pursuing justice. The warrior and battlefield metaphors have fed our furies far too long. It is not out of line to consider giving the image of God as War Lord a decent burial. It would take a community of believers to do this properly. But my monk decided to begin burial proceedings on

his own. I joined him over forty years ago and consider that to
be an amazing grace.

My marvelous maniacs
My friends in Viva House, the Catholic Worker House that
tends to the destitute in the inner-city of Southwest Baltimore
(Sowebo) and in Jonah House, were committed to promoting
civil disobedience. They encouraged me to hit the road and
walk the walk Jesus walked. More than anyone else they rudely
awakened me with their loud and startling chants:

Do something about peace and poverty.
Do it like Jesus did it.
Do it as if planet earth is to be God's kingdom.
Don't be a wimp about what you do.
Don't wallow in the lure of heaven.
Don't wallow in the fear of hell.

Jim, they said, you should be willing to suffer the
consequences of saying "no" to those who abuse power. They
have much to do with the least being the least. Deep in your
heart you know this. That is why the biblical stories of God and

Son saying "no" to the powerful touch our hearts so deeply. But in the real world we have yet to catch up with our stories. Our historical "no" to those who abuse power has been a wimpy and shameful "no". It has lacked the religious and political will to fit our actions to our favorite prayer: "Thy kingdom come on earth as it is in heaven."

My mother Church taught me to revere the story of Jesus as the victim of a mythological war between God and Satan. My marvelous maniacs insisted that Jesus was the victim of the ever-present and very real war between the mighty and the lowly. For them, and my monk, Jesus was the victim of the prediction made in the storied song of his pregnant mother. He was the victim of the war he waged in his ministry. He was the victim of his prayer about daily bread and a kingdom on earth.

Jim, they said, most believers in a kingdom on earth expect that God will get the kingdom job done all by himself, will do it "His" way. That belief is reflected in the first and last stories of the bible. God says let there be this and that, and that's how there was a garden of paradise. God descends with an apocalyptic fury saying let this be gone and that be gone and that's how there will be a kingdom of God on earth.

Whenever we have chipped in with our little kingdom on earth efforts we have relied primarily on bombs not bread. We have tried to be the spitting images of God's son as described in the last book of the bible. In that story there are only the good guys and the bad guys. The Christ leads an army of angels to wipe out the bad guys. That's the image and the story we have relied on. And we have been good at it – so far. We have become so good that we too have finally become like the storied Christ. We too can destroy the planet. The atomic clock is ticking. Time is running out on war as the solution to the kingdom on earth problem.

The war Jesus waged was the war to end all wars. He was The Man with a plan: put away the sword; love your enemies; put bread on every table; treat the least as you would treat me. This plan was not the ticket to heaven. If it were few of us would get to heaven. The Man with a plan gave us the ticket to peace on earth. His plan would put an end to civilization as humanity had known it since the dawn of civilization. His plan would make him the Prince of Peace, would reveal him as the beloved son of God. It was the plan Jesus and his cousin John called the kingdom of God on earth. Anything less than this plan would be unworthy of an incarnation of God dwelling among us.

It was because of these trustworthy friends that I tried to walk the Jesus walk. It helped that I always had had strong feelings about the poor. This came naturally to me.

My grandfather worked in the coal mines before there were unions. The work was hard and hazardous. On the way home some miners might stop in a bar. They would drop a raw egg in their beer to wash down the coal dust. Very often it was dark when they went to the mines, dark in the mines, and dark when they came home from the mines. My grandfather coughed his way into his coffin. The pay was poor. My grandmother supplemented his wages by transforming her living room into a grocery store.

My father came to this country as an illiterate boy, was wounded in the First World War, and never held down a decent job, except those part-time jobs provided by the Roosevelt administration. My mother supplemented our meager income by working in a cinder-block shirt factory, for meager wages.

While in grade school we lived in a two-room apartment above a bar, later a barber shop, two adults and two children with only an outhouse for a toilet. I was and always will be "bent" in favor of the poor. Everyone is bent in some way in matters that count.

I did the best I could as one bent in favor of the poor. I picketed with farm workers in California. I lived and worked in hospitality houses for the poor in D.C. I earned my living by digging graves and cutting grass in local cemeteries. I committed acts of civil disobedience against the war in Vietnam as part of the war against poverty. Twice I fasted on liquids only for forty days in protest of my bishop's position on the war. Twice I was arrested for acts of civil disobedience. I was tried in court both times but not convicted, though guilty as charged. Allow me to explain.

In trial number one I was one of about twelve protestors charged with blocking the entrance to Richard Nixon's Reelection Headquarters. The symbolism would be obvious. We wanted no more of Richard Nixon. The plan was simple. A small group, twelve if I remember correctly, would be chained together and ride in the back of a large van from our "headquarters" to Nixon's headquarters. On arriving we would leap out and each end of our human chain would lock onto the doors at each side of the lobby. Ta dah! Lobby locked down, headquarters sealed, point made.

I would like to tell you it was a well-executed maneuver but that would be a lie. The evening before the mission someone had borrowed the van and had not returned it. We had to walk to Nixon's headquarters, about three or four blocks away, chained in threes, all arriving from different directions. As my trio made its way we met two policemen coming our way. Our hands were in our pockets hiding the chains but it took a nifty little dance for our chained trio to sidestep them as the sidewalk was narrow.

Thanks be to God (dare I say that?) we got the job done. It helped that I had gone there the day before wearing my Roman collar, casing the place.

By law we were as guilty as sin, facing, if I remember correctly, six months in jail. But by the grace of God (dare I say that?) all the State's witnesses, the Nixon headquarters workers, were in the Bahamas celebrating Nixon's re-election. Case dismissed.

My second act of protest against the Vietnam War was less dramatic but just as illegal. During an open-to-the public tour of the White House a few of us broke from the tour line to kneel and pray. We prayed against a bombing that was supposedly the fiction of our unpatriotic imagination – the secret bombing of Cambodia. After being arrested, one secret-service agent lectured me. How can a priest desecrate the sanctity of the White House?

But by the time our case came to trial the judge was fed up with the war and with putting protestors in jail. He simply dismissed the case.

We had our weaknesses as does everyone. We made mistakes as does everyone. Not even angels could carry our attitude and live on the margins of society without losing some high ground. We were loud, pushy, single-minded and sometimes even haughty. But our mistakes paled before the mistake of a war that blasphemed God and Country.

My monk thought that the maniacs were the marvelous ones. He tended to be critical of himself. He wrote to Dorothy Day about his envy for her inner-city communities which lived with and worked with the poor. He saw them as a modern version of the earliest desert communities of monks. He was, of course, still committed to his monastic contemplation but he envied the hardy and helping character of their community life. She calmed him down. She shed a harsh light on her communities: "The poor and the voluntary poor can be bitter, critical, rebellious, and prone to see their rage as righteous." It was as if she had the eyes and heart of humility personified.

You can see why I count the monk and the maniacs as trustworthy friends. They held fast to a way of life that most believers cannot even imagine possible. They were open to self-criticism. "The Lords" on the other hand were always hesitant to self-criticize. They even tended to hide the heinous crimes of their clergy so that the laity would not be scandalized. If they had learned to think, talk, and live like my monk and maniacs I would not be favoring what my friends taught me about God over what they teach.

Being against the Vietnam War full throttle could get a priest into trouble with his bishop, even a priest given leave to work with the poor wherever he sees fit. I did get into trouble, not because of my arrests but because I gave communion to two anti-war activists who were living as husband and wife but were not validly married in the eyes of the church. I was living with them along with others who were promoting acts of civil disobedience. The two in question were Father Phil Berrigan and Sister Elizabeth McAlister.

Mass and communion meant a great deal to them. When asked to celebrate Mass I chose to respect their need for the sacrament of communion. They faced the possibility of jail every day and Phil eventually spent eleven years of his activist life in prison. The bishop (not the one I lived with but his successor) found out about our home mass, I still do not know how, and he ordered me to stop giving communion to Phil and Liz because they were invalidly married. I disobeyed him. Our liturgy was celebrated in the privacy of our home. We were not taking a public position against celibacy. We had enough on our plates as it was. We were only satisfying a spiritual need. When I refused to stop giving communion to Phil and Liz he ordered me back to the diocese. I disobeyed that order. Then he forbade me to function as a priest. I was well known in the area and my suspension made the headlines in the local paper: "La Croce takes a new view of the priesthood". The headline made me seem arrogant. But I suppose it was not totally out of line.

I had had it with the Bishop and he had had it with me. He was only too glad to be rid of me. With my consent he applied to the Vatican asking permission for me to live as a catholic layman. He did not mention the standoff between us about Holy Communion but only that I refused to return to work in the diocese as ordered.

Rome instructed the Bishop to allow me to continue the work that suited my temperament. That Rome saw the rightness of my ministry was an unexpected vindication of my life on the road. But I knew that once the standoff about communion was reported I would be in trouble with Rome.

I had already concluded that the best thing for me was to live the rest of my life as a layman rather than as a priest. So I wrote to Rome stating my personal reasons for wanting to leave the priesthood. I wrote in the strongest personal terms: "I am now experiencing graces of peace and joy which are amazing as they are mysterious. My living in a kind of limbo for such a long time has been a cross for my family, which accepted my decision to live as a layman only after a long and painful process. For their sake I want my status to be made formal and public as soon as possible."

In April 1976 I was "reduced to the lay state", granted permission to live as a catholic layman and given the right to marry in the Catholic Church. I did marry in 1980. My priesthood was a great grace, but the graces of living on the road and of getting married were even greater graces. My marvelous maniacs, my monk and my wife were the greatest of friends – they were the grace celebrated in Sirach 5: 14-16:

"Faithful friends are a sturdy shelter;
Whoever finds one has found a treasure.
Faithful friends are beyond price;
No amount can balance their worth.
Faithful friends are life-saving medicine..."

In ending this chapter I remember two of my uncles who fought in World War II, a war we still revere. In so doing I suggest that it is not out of line to consider giving the image of God as War Lord a decent burial.

Uncle Ralph: He was a favorite uncle. Long after he died we told Uncle Ralph stories at our family Christmas Eve dinners.

In World War II he fought in the South Pacific. He once told me that when they got off the boat in New York they should have kept their guns and marched right to Washington. I was shocked when he said that. Why did he feel so strongly against the government that sent him into war, a war we truly believed in? I said nothing because he fought in the war and I did not. My uncle was not a coward. One time two armed thugs entered his shoe repair shop to rob him. He yelled "Sonofabitch", slammed down his hammer on the counter, and these two bozos fled in fear. I loved my uncle. I think of him every time there is a war.

Uncle Ralph may have been angry because his youngest brother, Flory, was killed in the battle of the bulge – a battle that was fought after the war was just about over. My cousin Jimmy died in the same battle, in the same week.

Uncle Flory: He was the youngest of my uncles, only a few years older than me. He was easy going, full of fun and more like an older brother than an uncle. For a long time my grandmother refused to believe he was dead since she never saw the body.

I still have the letter my Uncle Flory sent to my mother and father a few weeks before he was killed. He wrote nothing about the killing field he was in. He apologized for not writing sooner:

"I had the time to write before but I wasn't in the writing mood. I can't explain it, all I can say is I'm sorry and I'll try not to let it happen again."

Then he asked about my brother and me, noting that my brother had written to him telling him I changed my name from Junior to Jimmy when I got into high school.

"I got a great kick at the way Gene told me, that Junior is becoming a Casanova – always talking to the girls."

He is in one of the bloodiest battles of the war and he gets a kick out my name change and me being a high-school Casanova.

This is war up close and personal. And I will never forget it. Never.

It's enough to make a grown man cry.

8. THE CABIN IN THE WOODS -
(Winter 1972- Spring 1977)

Jesus the Nazarene

"The true mystery of the world is the visible

not the invisible" (Oscar Wilde)

What can I say about my life on the road? It was the best of times. It was the worst of times. I was exhilarated. I was scared. I was flying by the seat of my pants. I was running with Jesus the trouble-maker. I was running as if the true mystery of faith was in the visible not the invisible. I was running without the bearings given to me as a devout Catholic and as a Catholic priest.

As a priest the light of my life was the Christ who took away the sin of the world. I made him present in the house of God, in the bread of life. As an activist the light of my life was the Jesus who ushered in the kingdom on earth. I made him present in White House and soup kitchens.

As a priest my faith was grounded on two tall stories:

1. Once upon a time God closed heaven because of Adam's one act of disobedience.

2. Once upon a time Satan said to God that there is no use opening heaven because no sinner will get there until you pay the blood ransom I demand before I release them from my power. After thinking it over God said OK to Satan because he had decided he would not open heaven anyway until his wrath was calmed by the bloody sacrifice of his son. In this tall story God and Satan agreed on the fate of Jesus: "There will be blood."

As an activist my faith was grounded on two very slim facts:

Jesus was sent to a real place in real time to minister to really oppressed people for whom life was a bitch.

Jesus was sent to be a personal pain in the butt to the mighty who made it so.

Theoretically my faith should enable me to live both by the stories and the facts. But it did not work out that way for me. While tending to the tall stories I tended little to the facts. While tending to the facts I came to believe that the facts and not the stories should be the foundation of my faith. This put me at odds with my family, friends and faith community. What I called tall stories they called sacred doctrines.

You have a lot of nerve, Jim, I told myself. You better get your act together. You need some quiet time. You need some alone time. You need a cabin in the woods.

I remember well my cabin in the woods. It was there that I tried to work out my conflict between tall stories and slim facts. I did plenty of writing in those days. Sometimes I wrote from dawn to dusk. What looked like a pen in my hands and felt like a pen was more like a scalpel in the hands of a clumsy surgeon. How could I be anything but clumsy? I wrote as one in a crisis of faith not as a potential author. What I wrote in the cabin stayed in the cabin and shared the same fate as the cabin. Nothing remains- except the indelible mark made on my soul, or the equivalent thereof.

My cabin was near the farmland some of my friends cultivated to provide food for the inner-city poor. It was at the bottom of a steep ravine. It was wrapped in silence.

It was a poorly wrapped habitat. I built it myself. I used discarded barn wood, old nails, and whatever windows I could scavenge to build one room with a small alcove for sleeping. The room was without heat, light and running water. It had only a barrel stove, a kerosene lamp and a nearby brook. It did not even have an outhouse. It did have a fireplace, built by a friend from Italy, the son of a diplomat.

I had what I most needed, a lamp for reading and writing and a fireplace for meditating.

Mid-point in building my cabin I asked a visiting priest friend how it looked. He asked whether I was putting it up or tearing in down. We laughed at his question. But like many a humorous remark, it hit the nail on the head.

It was in this cabin that I began to tear down the image of Jesus as the Christ and build up his image as the Nazarene. It was in this cabin that I revered the hard facts about Jesus rather than the tall stories about Christ. It was in this cabin that I confessed that the true mystery of faith is in the visible not the invisible:

The true mystery is in the word made flesh as a Jew. How odd of God to incarnate as a Jew. No pious Jew would, could, or should have revered Jesus as we do today, true God of true God, of the same divine substance as the Father. Nor did Jesus demand they do so.

The mystery is that the word made flesh wrongly believed that the kingdom of God on earth would take root in Galilee not in Galatia, and that it would take root thanks to the Jews not to the Gentiles. How odd of Jesus and Paul that they both got it wrong.

The mystery of mysteries is that treating "the least" as if they were Jesus did not make it into the creeds, the professions of faith, or the Sunday rituals of the followers of Jesus. Two thousand years after Jesus announced his mission to the least in his home synagogue "the least" still live a life that is a bitch and then it ends.

The mystery is in the hard facts about Jesus not the tall tales about Christ.

It is all so clear to me today but back in the cabin that was not the case. How could it be? My family name, La Croce, was a tribute to the cross. My ordination empowered me to re-enact

Jesus' crucifixion daily at the altar. My faith community
proclaimed that Jesus fulfilled his mission while on the cross
not while on the road. His mission was to get us into the
kingdom of heaven – even though his prayer to Our Father in
heaven suggests heaven is supposed to come to us, not the other
way round.

How could Jesus on the cross come to mean less to me than
Jesus on the road?

Why do I cherish a life that was suspect and dangerous over a
life that was devout and safe?

The answer my friends was my religious experience of Jesus
while on the road. In those years I was no longer the tradition-
minded and religiously well-positioned Pharisee described in
Luke 7:36-45. I was the sinful woman in that parable. I was the
woman who kissed the feet of Jesus. Oh how she loved those
feet. They kicked the least up a notch or two. They walked all
over the Lords. That is why the woman's kiss meant as much to
Jesus as it did to her. That is why the Pharisee did not know
what the hell Jesus was doing in preferring her kiss to his
fidelity to tradition.

While on the road I was that sinful tradition-breaking woman.
Kissing the feet of the road warrior made the worst of times the

best of times. Jesus had no reason to rebuke me as he did the Pharisee: "You gave me no kiss." For me, bending to kiss Jesus was a more rewarding religious experience than kneeling to adore Christ.

But could I live the rest of my life on the road? What would I do when the war ended? What would I do if I found out that I could not give the rest of my life to the least as Jesus did? How would I go about kissing the wandering feet of Jesus if I no longer walked with him, if I got a paying job, a house, a mortgage, a wife? Would my passion cool? Would his passion cool? The answer my friends came in the dark nights of the heavily wooded light-defying ravine where I had built my cabin.

The pitch-black nights were scary. You know what a wimp I am. Every little noise frightened me: What the hell was that? Worse yet, in the pitch-black darkness of those nights I was tempted to believe that I really had lost my bearings. I was scared, and in more ways than one.

But scary can become sacred when you least expect it. The night that it did was the night I saw how I could sustain my intimacy with Jesus even if I traded the road for the campus. Every lover knows that you cannot hug and kiss someone you have put on a pedestal. The heart of my experience of intimacy with Jesus was not being on the road but taking Jesus off the pedestal. I could do that and should do that if I left the road for the campus.

On campus I would say nothing about my life on the road. But what I taught would reflect those experiences. I would not promote the tall tales that put Jesus on the pedestal. What began on the road and in the cabin would continue on campus. Hugs and kisses would still be my way of relating to Jesus.

But how would "Campus Jim", teaching in a Roman Catholic College, go about taking Jesus off the Roman Catholic pedestal? It was not long before I came to see that it may be easier to do than I thought. Jesus had done much of the work for me.

1. Jesus lived thirty of his thirty three years in anonymity, off the pedestal.

2. Jesus appeared on the public scene as our worst nightmare,
as anything but a pedestal guy –a Jew who became the poster
boy for the dregs of society; a prophet who predicted that the
poor will inherit the earth; a judge who threatened with hell
those who did not treat the least as if they were Jesus.

If that is Jesus on a pedestal then I'm Napoleon.

3. Jesus never put himself on the pedestal as we love to do:
Not once did he say that he was the second person of a three-
person God; that he was conceived by a virgin mother, that he
was sent to open heaven, pay Satan's ransom demand, and
satisfy the wrath of his Father in heaven.

Not once did he tell any of the birth stories WE so dearly
prize – and rightly so, since they go so well with our Santa
stories. But Jesus' silence does tell us these are feel-good stories
not facts, or if they are facts they are not very important facts,
not pedestal-making facts. His silence cries out: "Would I not
be the revelation of God if conceived by sexual intercourse, if
my birth was not highlighted with a star, angels, kings and
slaughtered babies? Why not? All things are possible with God,
even God coming down off his high horse, even God living
with us as an off-the-pedestal incarnation. The incarnation we

believe in did not put him on a pedestal, as was the custom among the pedestal grabbing Gods and Goddesses in those days.

Whether on the road, in my cabin or on campus the facts were the same:

Second by second, minute by minute, hour by hour, day by day, month by month, and year by year Jesus lived out his incarnation in the slow motion of the anonymous and not at the warp speed of the almighty. In the thirty years or so of his hidden life he was off the radar screen.

And yet, if I had met Jesus in his anonymous life I suspect I may have greeted him with Max Brand's words: "That's a lot of man under one skin. You've tucked yourself into a quiet corner. Who are you going to scare when you pop out?"

When Jesus did appear on the radar screen he was quickly dealt with by the pedestal people. They stopped him from ushering in the kingdom of God on earth. They made his death a victory for the mighty in the everlasting battle between the mighty and the lowly. And a mighty victory it was. The proof is in the pudding of humanity today. The proof is also in the last words of Jesus, as reported by Matthew and Mark: "My God, my God, why have you forsaken me?" Would those be his last words if he believed that his cross was the key that opened heaven? I doubt it.

On the cross Jesus' last song was more Johnny Cash than Jesus Christ, more like country music than Gregorian chant. It was like those songs that come out of "starless nights on snake-black roads." Like the songs sung by the Man in Black, songs that remind us "that we're all lonely and all scared – but that we're somebody." In his song Jesus cries out: I'm not chopped liver, why have you forsaken me? These hands that fed and healed, these feet that took me to those most in need are now nailed to two planks of wood. I cannot bear the agony of this defeat!

Meanwhile, those who tell tall tales about the crucifixion still believe that Satan, after being paid the ransom he demanded, is to this day going about seeking whom he may devour. They still preach that the Father, after getting the pound of flesh he demanded, is as full of wrath as ever. Who can explain that? Who can tell me why? I don't even want to think about it.

My dark nights with Jesus were beginning to wear me down. The discomforts of my cabin began to take their toll - a barrel stove for heat, a kerosene lamp for light, no running water, and no outhouse. Worse yet, circumstances had caught up with me. The Vietnam War was winding down. My mission to the poorest of the poor was winding down.

Despite all my frantic running around and my high-minded running at the mouth about "the least" I had not found a way to give my life to their service. This should have been the time for self flagellation, as any zealot would tell you. But at the time I was too preoccupied to wallow in guilt. My work at the cemetery had taken a bad turn. I helped form a union there at the price of agreeing to leave. I found work in another cemetery but was bitterly resented by the other workers, all African-Americans except one. They resented the fact that I was allowed to work four days a week. They believed I was hired only to be a companion to the only white man on the crew. They made it tough for me. They were good at it because they were tough. They never laid a hand on me but they laid what they could on me. Working there was a daily strain.

Then, one day, by chance, they found out I had helped form a union in another cemetery. The union man they were meeting with spotted me and said: ask Jim about what he did to help start a union in the cemetery where he worked before coming here. Things eased up after that.

But I was now emotionally drained. I was pushing fifty, had been 'reduced' to the lay state, had fallen in love and was hoping to get married. I was now thinking less and less about protesting, about playing monk, and about the plight of the poor. I was thinking more and more about a paycheck. Somehow it did not seem right that a guy with a doctorate in theology, a teacher at heart, and a man planning to get married should be digging graves. Working in a cemetery was a dead-end job. My therapist was quick to point that out.

I had a lot on my plate. I needed a place with a bathroom nearby. More than that, I needed a job. Teaching would suit me quite well. Now that I was a Catholic layperson in good standing I could do what I had been trained to do and wanted to do. I wanted to teach theology. I wanted to teach in a Catholic College. I had a friend who taught at Catholic University in Washington. He told me not to apply. They would not hire a laicized priest, at least not to teach theology. Other applications were rejected. I knew someone at a small catholic college for women and applied there. The President, God bless her generous and hardy soul, was willing to hire me. Getting that job eased the shock of leaving my life on the road. I would be able to get married. I would be teaching theology.

Before I made the transition from cabin to city housing to campus I spent a week in prayer at a retreat house. I needed the time to sort out my guilt feelings about giving up my life on the road, my living with and working for "the least". That I was able to deal with these feelings so well is one reason I am ever so sensitive about not laying guilt trips on others. That is why the subtext of every word written in this book is simply this: listen but do not leap; do the best you can from where you are and with the hand that has been dealt you.

Coal miners dig for coal that contributes to global warming. Citizens serve a country that gobbles up most of the planet's goodies. Christians revere a book that has promoted sexism down through the ages. Catholics pledge obedience to a Pope who condemns them for practicing birth control.

Being without a job, a country, a bible, or a Pope can be a heavier burden than coal miners, citizens, Christians and Catholics could bear.

All we can do is do the best we can from where we are with the hand that has been dealt us. That's what I try to do. Even when I leaped forward in going on the road it was not long before I leaped back by getting off the road.

This book was conceived in the 1970's when I answered a question by asking a question. At that time I thought I had conceived more than a book. I thought I was being reborn into a new life of faith. I would live as another Jesus instead of as another Christ. My work day would be given to "the least" as another Jesus on the road rather than to "the faithful" as another Christ at the altar.

To my credit I gave this new life my best shot. Quiet Jim became loud-mouthed Jim. Obedient Jim was now disobedient Jim. Law-abiding Jim lived and worked with men and women who were considered unarmed but dangerous in North and South America. Polite Jim picketed with Migrant Farm Workers in California. Pasta-loving Jim twice fasted for forty days on liquids only in protest of his Bishops' support of the Vietnam War. Rectory-loving Jim lived in hospitality houses for the homeless. The Jim who once honored the dead by blessing their graves now dug their graves.

To my shame, after ten years on the road, I was neither another Christ (I had been laicized) nor another Jesus (I had not found a way to give my life to "the least"). The new life I thought I had conceived in 1970 was in danger of being aborted. But the president of The College of Notre Dame in Maryland, Sister Kathleen Feeley, saw to it that there would be no abortion. She dared to hire a laicized priest to teach Religious Studies. Not many Catholic Colleges dared to do that. Thanks to her, what had been denied me by my bishop when I returned from Rome was given to me by this nun when I left my life on the road.

But she did not know about my cabin in the woods. She did not know I had been influenced more by my teachers on the road than my teachers in Rome. She did not know that for me it was Passion or Perish not Publish or Perish. She did not know the questions I brought with me to her campus. She did not know that my cabin theology would not sit well with a Church hierarchy that clung to the belief that at the Last Supper Jesus founded the Last Holy Hierarchy – males only. These men had put Jesus on the highest possible pedestal. They proclaimed him as the Son of the CEO and architect of hell.

The president of the college knew nothing about my cabin. The priest friend who asked me if I was putting it up or tearing it down called me recently to tell me that where the cabin had once stood a rose bush now flowered. He was ribbing me of course. But for what happened to me in that cabin I would not have been surprised at such a sign of grace. I experienced some fierce and fiery graces in that cabin. If I had brought cabin Jesus into the classroom it would have burned the paint off the walls. Worse than that, it would have been unprofessional. Fire is for preaching. Enlightenment is for teaching.

I had to find a way to be true to my renewed self, fulfill my contract with the college and the students, and stay out of trouble with the local Cardinal, who happened to be my old pal Bill- the one who had offered me a promotion.

Meanwhile, back at the Vatican dark clouds were on the horizon.

9. PARDON THE INTERRUPTION -

Bad Uncle Jim

At this point in telling my story a dark voice within me is insisting on having a word with you. I call that voice "Bad Uncle Jim" – who, like "the devil", is a fiction called upon when saying or doing things which may be better left unsaid or undone. Bad Uncle Jim rants and raves about my being too soft on myself and on you. He doesn't care where I am in the story. He wants a crack at a few sacred cows.

The Lord's Day:
Exodus 20:11 tells us that Saturday not Sunday was set aside for rest not ritual sacrifice. Jesus told us that the Sabbath was made for man, not man for the Sabbath. The Church tells us we will go to hell if we do not attend the ritual sacrifice of the mass on Sunday. Go figure.

The Lord's Table:
The Pope recently said it is more reverent to kneel when receiving communion from the Lord's Table. I agree if you are receiving the bread as the body of Christ.

But it is better to receive the bread as the body of Jesus. Jesus was not yet the risen Christ when he said "this is my body." It was his body as the Nazarene that he shared with those at the last supper.

Why kneel when receiving the body of Jesus? Jesus would not know what to do if his friends and followers, all sinners by the way, knelt to receive him in their homes. If it is not the Pope who is giving you communion you are better off receiving the bread standing, receiving it as the body of Jesus.

The priest may give you the bread as the body of Christ but in your heart you should receive it as the body of Jesus.

The Lord's Books:

Do you believe God really behaves as described in the sacred books of the Jews, Christians and Muslims? How can this be since each claims God's presence favors them over all others? Is it possible that God's gracious presence is revealed more graciously in the unfolding of creation than in these books of revelation?

The Lord's Supper:

Twelve Jewish men sat at table with Jesus during Passover festivities. The twelve supposedly represented the gathering of the twelve tribes of Israel.

Jesus did not say the New Covenant meant the end of Judaism. If he did he was dead wrong.

My question to you: Was this a Jewish or Christian ritual? You tell me.

What did "this is my body" mean? Christians disagree so strongly that they refuse to eat at the same ritual table. Did those present take it to mean they were eating the flesh of Jesus under the appearance of bread? I doubt it. Their faith was in low tide. They were about to betray the real flesh and blood of Jesus.

What did Paul believe? Why did Paul have Jesus bless the bread as his body before the meal and bless the wine as his blood after the meal? Did he believe that the shared meal was an essential part of this ritual? Did he believe it was the sharing of food and drink that made Jesus present in a unique way? Is that why Paul was furious in learning that some had gobbled up most of the food and drink before the others arrived? Did he see it as more than bad manners and gluttony? If they could not share food and drink gracefully with each other what hope was there of them sharing it with the least? Was it with this in mind that Paul wrote: "Whoever, therefore, eats the bread or drinks the cup of the Lord in an unworthy manner will be answerable for the body and blood of the Lord." (1 Corinthians 11:27-34).

Would Paul scoff at the waxy wafer passed off as food in place of a real meal, a real honest-to-God sit-down meal shared with others, and especially with the least?

Was Jesus' last meal his final gift to the least? Was it his way of reassuring himself that the least would be fed after he died, fed as fully and gracefully as he fed them? Is that why his last wild and crazy parable made feeding the least our ticket to heaven, not feeding them our ticket to hell? If that is so could our ritual meals be more meals of condemnation than of salvation?

....

Bad Uncle Jim can really push the envelope. One time he came after me with his interpretation of the story of the tearing of the temple curtain when Jesus died. That was the curtain that kept hidden the special presence of God in the temple. Bad Uncle Jim's take was that God tore out of there as if He could not vacate the premises fast enough. Not even Jesus' prayer of forgiveness could stop him. Or so the Christian tradition would have us believe, he said snidely.

He then turned his full scorn on Christianity: Get real my fellow Christians! If you believe that story you better believe it can or has happened in your house of worship.

My response: You are an idiot – or worse. You take heartfelt stories probing at great mysteries so that you can mock them. Why not mock the talking, walking serpent while you are at it? God did forgive the few Jews who were responsible for his death on the cross, and the Italians (Romans) also. The Jews have been doing quite well without the temple, the altar sacrifices and the priests – even better than they did when they had them.

But since I was about to leave the cabin for the campus Bad Uncle Jim came at me with all the sarcasm he could muster:

Jim, you hope to teach in a College for Women. Good luck! God seems to be very touchy about being referred to as a woman. The first sentence of the bible could easily be: "Call me Lord, King, Father, or Master, and always refer to me as He or Him. Never call me Lady, Queen, Mother, or Mistress, and never refer to me as She or Her."

Few of your students will be unable to even imagine God as a woman. Good luck!

Jim, you hope to teach in a Catholic College. Good luck! The portrait of God in the bible fits the Oxford dictionary definition of "touchy":

"Easily moved to anger, apt to take offense on a slight cause, highly sensitive in temper and disposition, irascible, irritable, testie, titchy."

When reading many a biblical passage the seventeenth century text cited in the Oxford dictionary comes to mind:

"Ther's the old tutchie, testie Lord!"

Good luck!

Before being rudely interrupted by Bad Uncle Jim I was telling you about my dilemma. In moving from the cabin to the campus I had to find a way to be true to myself and my students. I also noted with some concern that meanwhile, back at the Vatican, dark clouds were on the horizon. The church had been interpreting revered traditions in light of Vatican II. Now the Vatican began to interpret Vatican II in light of revered traditions.

10. ON A CATHOLIC COLLEGE CAMPUS - (Early 1980's)

The Son's divinity? - The Father's Hell?

Pondering in a cabin is one thing. Teaching in a classroom is something else. Road Jim and Cabin Jim had to give way to Campus Jim and married Jim. No more acts of civil disobedience, no more living in hospitality houses. No more trying to live as if "the least" are more precious to Jesus and his mission than are the rest of us. But Cabin Jesus would have to show up on campus in some way. And indeed he did.

While in the woods I learned to revere Jesus as showcasing his humanity not his divinity. I could easily imagine God saying to Jesus: do not mess up. No showing off. No walking across Herod's swimming pool.

Roman Catholic Teaching revered Jesus as showcasing his divinity. It would have us believe that Jesus did this also. Yes, the Church teaches that Jesus was truly human as well as truly divine. But her creeds, doctrines and rituals overshadow the human Jesus. All the important jobs were done by Jesus as the Christ, Jesus as the same divine substance as the Father, Jesus as the spitting image of his Father, not by Jesus as the Nazarene, Jesus as one of us.

The most important job in the hands of Jesus as the divine Son of God, as "the Christ", was seeing to it that his followers ended up in heaven rather than in hell. The kingdom on earth job begun by "the Nazarene" was gradually devalued. That is why the followers of Jesus were eventually called "Christians" not "Nazarenes."

As a rookie teacher in a Roman Catholic College I had a problem. The Jesus I experienced on the road was nothing like the Jesus showcased in our tradition, nothing like the Father showcased in the bible.

What was I to do?

The Son's Divinity?

How could a rookie teacher address this problem? How could I translate my experiences to my students? How could I explain Jesus as a son who behaved nothing like the God described in the bible?

The bible tells us that God flooded the world in a fit of anger. Can you imagine Jesus flooding Galilee in a fit of anger? I cannot. I do not even believe Jesus caused a storm on the Sea of Galilee just to teach his disciples a lesson. If he did it was a miracle wasted.

God sent Moses to Pharaoh with ten plagues in his hip pocket: "See, I have made you (like) a God to Pharaoh." (Ex. 7:1) Can you imagine Jesus playing the role of Plague-Meister to Pilate? I cannot. That would have betrayed his commitment to non-violence.

The Jesus I experienced in my life on the road was not the spitting image of God as described in the bible. He was no War Lord. He would turn the other cheek rather than strike a blow. He was not the kind of son who could take over his father's business. I cannot imagine Jesus running hell without breaking into tears.

How Jesus could be so unlike the biblical portrait of his father and still be revered as his Son is an issue I would have to deal with.

I was forced to meet the issue of a Son unlike the Father when assigned to teach an introductory course on the bible. This was a course all students had to take. The textbook I selected was entitled: "And God Said What?"

The author raised some hard questions about the biblical portrait of God. She encouraged her readers to read the bible as a library of story books about God. She noted that these stories were told around campfires for ages and ages before being put into writing. Then they were copied for ages and ages before finally becoming "the bible". If some day any of my Christian students experienced Jesus as I did, as an "ungodly" son so to speak, the shock could be manageable. They would come to see that Jesus was not unlike God but was unlike the sacred but primitive stories told about God. They might even come to see that Jesus being so unlike this primitive portrait is what his followers should revere as the fullest revelation of God and of how God goes about being God on planet earth.

But some students were startled to hear me ask: "Did God say that? Did God do that?" They were uneasy when I characterized biblical texts as religious fiction – inspired yes, but as stories not as facts. I reminded them that the Genesis accounts of

creation in six days and of a world flood in forty days could not
be factual. I often reminded them that in a college course on
God they could not leave their intellect outside the classroom.
This was a classroom not a Church. I was standing at a lectern
not a pulpit.

I told them that the accounts of God making instant adults and
a talking serpent could be factual. But I suggested that the
correct question was not whether God could do these things but
whether God ever did such things.

Did God allow evil into a garden of paradise, located in what
is now Iraq, by way of a talking serpent? Or is that just a story?
If it is a story why did Christian missionaries laugh at primitive
South Americans for their sacred story about evil coming into
the world by way of a dog escaping from a legendary jungle
swamp? They said it was because the dog story is based only on
"folk-lore". The serpent story is a "revelation" in a book
inspired by God. The bible is God's book.

I found a dramatic way to challenge their unexamined piety
about the bible as God's book. The next day I entered the
classroom holding the bible high above my head, tossing these
verbal grenades, breaking up their class chatter:

Have you read God's book from cover to cover? How often have you done this?

In reading God's book are you overwhelmed by every word as inspiring, as divine? Or are you sometimes bored and confused?

Why have so many bible believers fought over the meaning of the bible; the Pharisees against the Sadducees; the Christians against the Jews; the Protestants against the Catholics; the liberals against the fundamentalists?
Why is it that the only clear-cut good vs. evil conflict over the meaning of the bible was between Satan and Jesus?
Each quoted the bible to prove his point.

If the bible is by God and about God why do Catholics pay more attention to the teaching of the Church? Why do Fundamentalist teachers spend so much time interpreting and explaining what God wrote? The more fundamentalist they are the more bible classes they have. Was God clumsy and inept in explaining himself?

131

Why was most of God's book written in Hebrew and for the Jews? Why did God stop "his" revelations? Why no more additions to the bible?

Could it be that "revelation" is not grounded on words from God but on myths and legends? Could it be that the revelation is but the "religious imagination" doing the work assigned to it by God and doing it under God?

Could it be that the most cherished Christian belief should be that God spoke only one word? Could it be that one word was "Jesus"?

Some students were uneasy and others were shocked at these questions. I told them I expected no answers but asked only that they keep their minds open when comparing the dog in the swamp story with the serpent in the garden story.

Once I had their attention I settled into the main theme of the course: To have a life with God we have no choice but to rely on stories. We have no data to compute and analyze – no quotations, no sightings. That is why our book about God is primarily a book of stories. Our bible is one story after another:

Once upon a time there was a garden with two instant adults, two magic trees and a walking/talking serpent; once upon a time God flooded the world and wiped out every living thing except for one family and its menagerie; once upon a time God took away humanity's common language because the people of Babel built a tower that reached heaven; once upon a time God started a special human family by having a hundred year old man impregnate a woman well past her childbearing age; once upon a time God allowed a Pharaoh to laugh off nine plagues so that he could send a child-killing plague that the Pharaoh could not ignore; once upon a time God opened up heaven by using a virgin to incarnate flesh destined to be nailed to a cross, etc., etc., etc.

I pointed out that the bible's reliance on stories was in keeping with a deep-seated human instinct. Even in our data-oriented secular lives stories play a crucial role. David Mamet, playwright and script writer, explains why:

"It is human nature to impose narrative structure
on our lives, as a way to invest otherwise random
events with meaning .... as pointing to

and providing a 'cleansing sense of awe'".

No doubt about it! We are not robots. We live and have our being in remembered stories, not in data as computed and analyzed. Whenever there is meaning and awe in our lives there are stories.

How could it not be so in our life with God? There are no meaning-making facts or data to go by. There are only meaning-making stories. Our God stories are stories of the people, by the people and for the people. They are intended to promote the faith of the people who hold them to be sacred. They are stories of people in primitive times doing the best they can with what they have. I tried to make this point again and again in my introductory course. In this way I could open my students to seeing Jesus as "ungodly" and yet not be disoriented.

I kept telling myself that they could take heart in knowing that Jesus was not unlike God but unlike the sacred and primitive stories about God. They could freely and easily celebrate Jesus' decision to be the nail rather than the hammer, to be a suffering rather than a punishing presence.

But my plan hit a snag when I was assigned to teach a course on Jesus.

Pope John Paul II had just issued an encyclical. It opened with these words: "The redeemer of man, Jesus Christ, is the center of the universe and of history." The Pope highlighted the divinity of Jesus. In the bible the Father was revered mostly as the center of Israel. In the encyclical the Son is referred to as the center of the universe. Giving Jesus a dominion much larger than that of the Father clearly highlighted the divinity of Jesus.

A long standing church tradition declares that Father and Son are 'of the same divine substance' (whatever that may mean). Some early Fathers of the Church claimed that to even question 'the sameness' of Father and Son could destroy Christianity. Given that long standing and resolute insistence it's a wonder no impious wag ever wise-cracked: How odd of God to be a Jew?

What was I to do with my course on Jesus? I did not want to be accused of attempting to destroy Christianity, unlikely as it was that any course I taught could endanger the Christian tradition.

I was in a bind. If I highlighted Jesus as the same divine substance as the father how would I draw my students to the Jesus who was not at all like the biblical portrait of the Father?

What was I to do? How would I share my experience of Jesus in teaching the course assigned to me?

The answer, my friends, was stunningly simple. How it came to me I cannot say. Whether it came the second, third or fourth time I taught my Jesus course I do not recall. But at one of my lectures I surprised myself as well as my students. I announced, in a light-hearted fashion, that I was going to place "the divinity" of Jesus on the classroom windowsill. I went through the motions of lifting "the divinity" from the lectern and walking, palms upward, carrying it to the windowsill behind me. There I ceremoniously placed "the divinity" out of sight-and out of mind. Returning to the lectern I declared that the divinity of Jesus would have no place on my lectern or in our class discussions.

I assured the students that we were not denying the divinity of Jesus (whatever that may mean) but only ignoring it. It's about time we gave Jesus' divinity a rest, I said. It has been overworked down through the centuries. I was on firm ground in saying this. One of our best theologians said it was high time we gave full and undivided attention to the humanity of Jesus. One of our most respected biblical scholars said that, biblically speaking, it is more accurate to say that Jesus is the revelation of God, than to say Jesus is God. Some Jesus scholars saw great value in emphasizing the humanity of Jesus. They were making research breakthroughs in their search for the historical Jesus. Scholars were now studying and discussing Jesus as one of us rather than as one of the Trinity.

Questioning hands sprang to life:

Can't we talk about the miracles of Jesus? Of course, his miracles do not prove his divinity. Moses and Peter performed miracles.

What about his title "Son of God"? That does not prove his divinity. God directs Moses to tell Pharaoh that "Israel is my Son, my first born..." (Ex. 4: 22).

My lectures went something like this.

Nothing highlighted the humanity of Jesus more than Jesus at prayer. God does not pray to God. The more Jesus prayed the more he saw himself as human rather than as divine.

The way Jesus lived when not at prayer also highlighted his humanity. He increased in wisdom as he grew older. He was known as the carpenter's son and did not object to be called such. He enjoyed his good days and lamented his bad days. He endured temptation. He avoided the adulation of those who believed in him as much as possible.

His contemporaries were not even tempted to revere him as true God of true God. They were all pious Jews, strict monotheists. No story about Jesus has any of them falling on their knees in his presence.

Only after the story of his "resurrection appearances" (whatever that may mean) does Thomas drop to his knees saying: "My Lord and my God." Jesus as the Nazarene would not have put up with such shenanigans. He lived his life as one of us. He loved living it as one of us. He died living it as one of us. Why that counts for so little in our creeds and doctrines is beyond me. Why we make such a big issue of the divinity of Jesus when Jesus did not is beyond me.

The stories about Jesus' way of being present were so unlike the stories about the way "The Father" was present.

1. The Father lived and had his being as one enthroned, not so the Son.

Jesus was born, as the story goes, into royal lineage but he made no claims to royalty. In his day the only Israelite royalty was the High Priesthood. He could not even become an ordinary priest because he was not of the priestly lineage. He did not seek the official status of "rabbi" – even though, as the story goes, he showed off his knowledge of the Torah as a teenager.

2. The Father could not stand the stench of sin. One time he flooded the world to get rid of it. Stories of the son tell us that he ate and drank with sinners, healed them, no problem.

3. The father instructed his chosen people to live by the sword. The son, so the story goes, said that those who live by the sword die by the sword. He never carried a sword or even a dagger. He never slapped a face. Indeed, he told his followers that when slapped they should turn the other cheek. His weapons were his words. The best of them were short stories called Parables.

4. The Father seemed to live by the rule "Publish or Perish". Sacred tradition would have us believe that he wrote in stone and dictated a book to Moses. He saw to it that "it is written" became the most sacred utterance among his people. The Son wrote nothing. He could have ordered his apostles to see that his words were duly recorded whenever he spoke, publicly or privately. He could have commanded this be done within days and weeks. Instead it was decades before anything was put in writing. By then only remembrances of his words remained, not the very words themselves. He did not care. His remembered words would be written in Greek, not Aramaic. He did not care. It was as if his words mattered only in the moment spoken, and only to the persons to whom they were spoken. The Son seemed to see his words as being of limited value, not worth disseminating outside his little circle. He saw them as "sown seeds" not "stone monuments."

He did write, as the story goes, but only once and only on the ground. He quickly rubbed out his words, as if embarrassed by this momentary lapse.

5. The father was conventional in relying on lording as the solution. The son was unconventional in relying on serving as

the solution. The son could have been a Lord like his father. He had those crowd-pleasing skills which go so well with "lording". He could tell a story, he could heal, he could stand up to power, and he had charisma. But "lording" was not his goal. He did not seek an office, titles, money, or anything that would give him lordly power. He would have nothing to do with any power but the power of serving the least. He had nothing to do with any status that did not allow – did not favor - his eating and drinking with sinners. He ate and drank in the leisurely intimacy of reclining at the table, as was the custom in those days. One can imagine that a good time was had by all.

How in the name of God could the son be so unlike the father – without being disinherited?

I can imagine the Torah-toting Father breaking in on his Son eating and drinking with sinners and shouting: "Jesus, you are so busted! And what is this business of saying 'it has been said but I say?'" Yes indeed, I can imagine a Torah-toting Father making such a fuss.

I can imagine Jesus using his dying breath to cry out "My God" instead of "Father". I can imagine him asking himself: "Should I have called on the twelve legions of angels at the ready? Should I have crushed those who came to arrest me? Should I have acted more like my father? Have I forsaken my Father? Has my Father forsaken me? Am I really his Son?" Yes, I can imagine Jesus as a man on a mission bitterly lamenting his crucifixion.

I can imagine Israel and Islam, in good faith and in the grace of God, rejecting Christianity's claim that Jesus is the son of God. Moses and Mohammed acted more like the biblical God than Jesus. They laid down laws, they were warriors, they were ruthless if need be. They did not settle for being pushed around in an ungodly way.

I can imagine Christianity, in good faith and in the grace of God, celebrating Jesus as "the Christ" rather than as "the Nazarene." No surprise there. The Christ is the spitting image of the biblical portrait of the Father, enthroned in power as both King and Judge.

I can imagine the three great revelation religions, in good faith and in the grace of God, favoring and abiding in the image of

God as an almighty and fearsome power. Is it not true that Humanity has always looked to power rather than love in solving its problems? That its sacred stories would revere God as a powerful presence is understandable.

But after living with God and Son for over seventy years I have come to imagine the Son's presence as being relational more than judgmental, healing rather than punishing, oriented to this world rather than the next.
And I have come to believe the Son is the fullest revelation we have of the Father's presence.

That was the message I tried to share with my students on a Catholic College Campus. It was not easy. On campus I was a theologian not a troubadour. In preparing my courses I could not dismiss the voices of my professors in Rome. They were the best teachers my Church had to offer. The voice of "Roman Jim" constantly berated "Road Jim".

Roman Jim:

You were trained to be a theologian. Theology highlights
Jesus as the Christ not as the Nazarene: Jesus bred to a life of
divine power by his virginal conception; Jesus sent to open
heaven by shedding blood as true God of true God; Jesus
glorified as the risen, ascended and ruling Christ. Are you
proposing Christianity without Christ? You sound like that
nutcase in one of Flannery O'Connor's wild stories.

Road Jim:

Hey, don't knock nutcases. God writes straight with crooked
lines. Besides, Jesus' followers led a godly life without a Christ.
They prayed only to the Father, as Jesus taught them to pray.
They learned by parables not creeds. They were taught to
reverence the least not the lords. There was only an occasional
obscure reference to "the Christ" – so obscure that even Peter
got it wrong. When they wrote their stories about Jesus they
focused on Jesus on the road not Jesus in the clouds.

It is the human Jesus who imposes the final narrative structure
on how God goes about being God on planet earth.

But even stronger than those two inner voices were the voices of my students. Because of them I taught more than I knew. They always asked the right questions. One I remember so well: "Doctor La Croce, how far will you go in stressing the humanity of Jesus? Was he as sexual as any Jewish male of his time?

I responded that the critical challenge of our faith is not the full divinity but the full humanity of Jesus. We find it hard to go all the way in confessing Jesus' humanity. Surely the body of Jesus sweated, broke wind, voided waste matter as do our bodies. Having been taught that Jesus was conceived without sex we tend to see him as sexless. We find it hard to imagine that Jesus had any sexual drive whatsoever – that his body did what all male bodies do when aroused. Surely as a Jewish adolescent Jesus had a heart that skipped a beat when Rachel, Rebecca, Miriam, Sarah and others smiled at him, teased him, asked him to help carry their water jugs, danced with him at the weddings they attended and sat near him around the camp fires when traveling to other villages. Surely Jesus did not walk through adolescence as a robot, a geek, an emotionally deprived loner. What kind of incarnation would that be? It would hardly be a reasonable facsimile of the glory of human sexuality as designed and created by God.

We presume Jesus did not have sexual intercourse because he was not married. He did not marry because of his vocation not because he had no sexual feelings or desires. It was no sin for Jesus to have and to hold dearly his romantic inclinations even though they were packaged in his sexual arousals. These spontaneous movements are not intrinsically evil. There is no hint in the creation story that Satan put the sexual drives in the bodies of Adam and Eve when God wasn't looking. Sexual feelings are part of God's plan. Thank God that humanity has been so graced that a look, a smile, a wave, a touch, a kiss, an embrace can cause a heart to leap with joy. Yes, humanity has abused the gift of sex but no more than it has abused the gifts of power, faith, and planet earth.

My heart once leaped precipitously at a smile, a leap that changed my life. Jesus took a different path than the one I finally took after that look. But how many fires did he sit around sharing and receiving smiles from women who worked and walked with him in his ministry? He may or may not have kissed Mary Magdalene on the lips. If it was the custom then as it is among friends today then I suspect he did. I expect they were able to handle it without betraying themselves. Do not forget, Mary was the first one Jesus greeted in the story of that wonderful Sunday morning.

Each time Jesus' divinity was raised by a student I reminded her to put it on the windowsill where, in this course, it would always remain. For all I know the divinity of Jesus may still be on the windowsill of classroom G315. Then again, it may be back on the lectern. Since I retired the Vatican has increased its vigilance over classroom lectures. I may have gotten out of there in the nick of time.

The Father's hell?

For two thousand years Christians were led to believe in hell and to believe that hell was here to stay. Prophets, parables, popes, preachers, and poetry - not to mention the music still played in the great concert halls, the art displayed in museums, the manuscripts preserved in libraries fed this belief in one way or another. Of course, Jesus' references to hell played a key role in the belief that God is the architect and CEO of an underground pit commonly called hell.

The hell-fire tradition is a chilling tradition, the highly prized "revelation" of Judaism, Christianity and Islam, thank you very much. Taking it seriously one could easily conclude that many of God's children ended up in hell. Saint Augustine at times referred to "the damned masses". Christians had to learn to live with the fear of hell, with a God whose life was 'Satan-centric.' God and Satan seemed to be always at war over our souls. Yes Virginia, there is a hell. As sure as God made little green apples God made hell. That's how I was raised.

For those of us who grew up in that tradition our dismay is that our childhood fear of hell may be hard wired. Will it still plague us on our death bed?

I was doing well as a teacher, having been honored as distinguished teacher of the year, by vote of faculty and students. This is not as awesome as it may sound. But the award did push me to work harder in living up to the saying by Clifford Geertz: "A scholar can hardly be better employed than in destroying fear."

But first I would have to destroy fear in myself before trying
to do it in a classroom. I began by allowing myself to get in
touch with my anger about hell. It went something like this:

Hell and I:

I do not thank you, mother church, for raising me to live in
fear of eternal torment. I do not thank you for your appalling list
of "go to hell" sins. I am not now nor ever have been a
notorious sinner. But I was raised by you to live with the fear of
going to hell. I lived with this fear while trying to be a healthy
adolescent. Every unchecked impure thought, word or deed
was a "hell-worthy" sin. Any one of them could send me there
if I died before confessing it to a priest. I accepted this as right
and just because that's what I had been taught by trusted
teachers – who were taught by trusted teachers, all relying on
the trusted Bible, to teach us what we trusted to be God's rules
for the game of life. The number one rule for me as an
adolescent was this: put an airtight lid on sex or live under the
threat of eternal torture. Case closed. And yet, I could hardly
take this rule and this threat literally. If I allowed the fear of
hell to work its terrible logic to its logical conclusion I would
have been a basket case. All catholic adolescents in my

adolescent world would have been basket cases – especially the males. Who in his right mind would risk eternal pain for one act of masturbation? And yet, who in his right mind would try to stop every erection in its tracks? Some of them were like runaway locomotives.

I suspect that God did for me what Twain did for Huckleberry Finn. Finn believed he would go to hell if he did not return his friend, nigger Jim, to his rightful owner. He tore up the note informing Jim's owner where Jim was hiding, holding his breath and saying to himself: "All right, then, I'll go to hell." Twain had Finn risk hell rather than betray nigger Jim. Somehow, God enabled me to risk hell rather than betray adolescent Jim. Who else but God could have helped adolescent Jim live with the fear of eternal punishment?

Unfortunately, I did not realize that learning to live with the fear of God did not help my learning to live with the love of God. This is no small matter since love is the name of the game of life created by God. I had no idea how destructive was the threat of hell. I do not thank you, mother Church, for your part in this.

Hell and my mother:

Nor do I thank you, mother Church, for your part in making life more difficult for my mother Mary. She was not a notorious sinner, nor scrupulous about sin, but she was a hell-fearing Roman Catholic. She once told me of her fear of hell. How could this be I asked her? You endured a most difficult husband-wife relationship but did not divorce. You were both bread winner and housewife but did not grumble. You were paid low wages for your work in a cinderblock shirt factory, but did not skimp on feeding and clothing us. You put healthy and tasty food, and I do mean tasty, on our table and clean clothes, and I do mean clean, on our backs, spotlessly clean and well-made clothes, even though money was scarce. Mostly on your own you raised two sons to live their lives in the sight of God. You had a hard life but never lost your sense of humor, never lost your sense of faith.

You go to Mass on Sunday, receive communion, pray the rosary and have devotion to the Saints. Your favorite prayer is "Little Flower in this hour show thy power."

Clearly you are a devout believer and a good mother. How could you even think for a moment that God would put you in Hell?

What I said to her helped for a time. Still, I could see that the fear was still there. But I did not feel free to probe any further. I was her son not her priest. However, I did come to understand her fear. In that long list of praise of my mother one item of praise was the good job she did in raising two sons under difficult circumstances. This glory was also her grief. She had only two children. She practiced birth control. This choice should not have been a problem. My father had been dead for many years. My mother had confessed this "sin" and could "sin" in this way no more. But I had a strong hunch as to why this fear may still have troubled her. It was her inability to be truly sorry that she had gone against the official teaching of the Church. She must have felt she did the right thing in having only two children. She could not truly repent. I'm guessing here, but it is not a wild guess. As a priest I had heard confessions and came across the same unresolved tension. I often heard these words in confession: "I believe I'm doing the right thing, Father, but the Pope says this is a mortal sin." It angered me no end to see my mother suffer this fear, even if only sporadically.

In my mother's final years the pain of cancer was a cross laid on her by her body. The fear of hell was a cross laid on her by her Church. I do not thank you, mother Church, for your part in making life and death more difficult for my mother Mary.

Hell and the College Campus:

Nor do I thank you, mother church, for making my life as a religion teacher more difficult. I felt compelled to include our belief in Hell in my course on the Christian Religious Experience. The doctrine of hell is right smack in the heart of Christian tradition. It had to be addressed in a Roman Catholic college. Hiding our hell tradition was not an option for me.

For almost 2000 years the threat of hell, the tortures of hell, the sins that put believers in hell, had been trumpeted by the Christian Church in its dogmas and creeds; in its poetry, folklore, art and music; in its churches, colleges, catechisms and creeds.

Most of our students were raised to believe that God took their sins personally, took them as a deliberate rejection of his love. To die in sin meant the cancellation of their invitation to live with God in heaven. God wanted nothing to do with them. The ticket to heaven became a ticket to hell. I had to address this teaching. I must confess, I did so more as a preacher than as a professor.

A helluva task:

I gave my students readings from ancient texts and modern literature describing and lamenting the never ending tortures of hell. I asked them if they believed any sin or crime could justify such tortures. A female student cried out "rape". You could hear a pin drop. I had no idea what to do. I knew what I wanted to say but I was afraid I would shock my students. I let the silence lie there for some time then I dismissed the class.

I knew I had to find a way to deal with that outcry and that silence. I decided to throw at them the same kind of verbal grenades I used in challenging the long held tradition about the bible. At the next class I entered the classroom tossing at them the following explosive questions:

What kind of God has a final solution for sinners that is more cruel than Hitler's final solution for the Jews?

What kind of God weakens his children with the mark of original sin but allows Satan his full power?

What kind of God allows confusion to prevail about the list of "go to hell" sins? Who can tell which list is being followed: the Jewish, Roman Catholic, Protestant or Muslim?

What kind of God needs hell in order to move us to know, love, and serve him in this world so we can be happy with him in the next?

What kind of believers are we if we call this kind of God "merciful father, just judge"?

The students, stunned and bewildered asked: "Dr. La Croce, how would you answer these questions?" I was evasive. At first I told them that these questions were intended to keep them from being close-minded about our discussion on hell. Being close-minded is a tendency which I deplore as a college teacher. But in reality these questions were expressions of my rude awakenings about the portrait of God given to me by my Church: touchy about sin and incredibly cruel in punishment. Gradually I no longer held back my anger about Christianity's teaching on hell. I flat out declared that it is an amazing disgrace. It is a godforsaken tradition that tries to portray God as a loving father who claims that vengeance belongs only to him. It is a sorry tradition that calls eternal torture justice rather than vengeance. What justice is there in an almighty God inflicting everlasting pain on pitifully weak humans – no matter how much grace God gives us or how evil we may have been. Just because there was a Hitler does not mean there must be a hell.

A strange God, indeed: a supposedly loving God with an eternal torture chamber in the basement of the world. He claims to be totally different and yet gets the job done the good old fashioned way, fear and punishment. He craves the reassurance of being the CEO of hell: without hell I just could not get the job done! Without hell I would get no respect. With hell I can get the respect I deserve: "I can punish you any way I please and as long as I please." In light of this teaching God becomes a hulking, sulking, vengeful presence in our lives.

Is this what the images of God should expect to hear when they first meet face to face: "My child, death brought you to me with mortal sin on your soul? I can't stand the sight of you. Go to hell."

Why can we not imagine God saying: "If that is the best you have done so far then keep working on it. I will find a way for you to do so. Physical death is not the deadline – no pun intended."

Such an option is called reincarnation in the East. We Catholics have a belief something like that in our tradition. It is called purgatory. Why certain sins should send us straight to hell instead of purgatory is beyond me.

I was becoming less and less convinced that our teaching on hell served any useful purpose. We who lived under its threat were not much different from those who did not. As a hell-believing community we have been as hard-hearted and mean-spirited as those who do not share this belief – perhaps even more so. Those who do not believe in hell have not had any reason to exclaim: "See how the fear of hell makes them a holy people, see how it helps them to love one another, see how it helps them treat the least as if they were Jesus."

In my lecture I made it clear we were speaking about the New Testament portrait of God. The Hebrew Torah pictured God as flooding the world, killing Egyptian babies and committing acts of violence too numerous to mention. The Hebrew Prophets pictured God as resurrecting only the Just, returning the wicked to the dust of the earth, not to hell. The New Testament portrait is hardly that of a kinder and gentler God, especially in its last book. In it planet earth becomes hell on earth before it becomes the kingdom of heaven, with only a remnant being saved by Christ.

In the last book of the Christian bible God is the image and likeness of us at our worst. He is driven by the emotion of being pissed off. If you want to know what pissed off means read "Revelations." And yet the pissed off tradition of God's apocalyptic fury has flourished for over 2000 years.

The believers who lived and died believing in hell are too numerous to count. One wonders how many could have been blessed with a happy death. No wonder popular Catholic piety embraced a somewhat magical way of avoiding hell. I refer to the practice of receiving communion on the first Friday of nine consecutive months. To do this gave assurance that you would not end up in hell.

The thought of meeting such a God, face to face, even if "He" welcomed me into heaven, terrifies me. What if some of my family and my friends were in hell? How could I love him for that? How could I love the architect and CEO of a place of eternal torture? How much could I love a God who handicapped my growth in love by stressing obedience to laws everyone breaks some way or other and threatens me with unbelievable torment? If God made me to love him in this world and in the next, then the threat of hell is, it seems, most ungodly.

Hell and the Pope:

Is the Pope Catholic? That was my reaction to an interview an Italian journalist had with Pope John Paul II. In it the Pope said that God has never revealed "whether or which human beings" are eternally damned. "I'll be damned! Is the Pope Catholic?" was my first reaction. Can the Pope say we do not know "whether" anyone is in hell; that hell is not a place where God tortures sinners; that only those who refuse to love God suffer the torment of not living with God; that one may ask if such a refusal is even possible? Can the Pope speak of hell in this way? Apparently he can and did. At least that is the way I read this informal interview.

Others have spoken of hell this way but there is nothing better for a catholic than hearing it from the lips of the Pope. True, the setting of the Pope's statement was informal and his words have yet to be given full papal prominence. Hopefully his statement on hell is not an "obiter dicta" – something said in passing, incidentally, and not well thought out. In any case it is no small matter for a Pope to speak about hell as he did.

The current Pope, Benedict XVI, was recently quoted as saying that there is a hell and it is eternal. But I don't think he would go as far as Pope Benedict XII who made this solemn definition in 1336:

"We further define that in accordance with God's universal ordinances the souls of those who die in actual mortal sin descend immediately after death to hell where they are tormented by eternal punishment."

Hell and the third millennium:

Many Catholics today pay no mind to the traditional teaching on hell. They do not see their so-called mortal sins as a rejection of God's love. They go further than the Pope on this. They go to communion without going to confession – though surely they commit the same sins we old-time Catholics had to confess before taking communion. They go to communion in good faith, as spiritually weak and in need of nourishment not as sinless and full of grace. As noted earlier they might do well to receive the blessed bread as the body of Jesus who ate and drank with sinners rather than as the body of Christ.

When I was young the communion lines were short. Today most of the congregation takes communion, birth-control, divorce, etc. notwithstanding. I was not surprised to read recently that this practice has been admonished by the Vatican. Of course, the Vatican has yet to warn us about taking communion even though we have not treated "the least" as if they were Jesus. Nor should it, given the way we were raised in the faith.

The likelihood of dying without the terrorizing fear of hell is on the rise, for you and for me. My nieces and nephews, my grandnieces and grandnephews, my step-grandchildren, and, above all, my godchild, will not be burdened with the fear of hell. If my mother were her own great granddaughter she would not have been so burdened. The Church in the third millennium should be, hopefully, a hell-free zone.

Saying goodbye to hell is the first step in saying goodbye to God as an almighty presence.

The ticket to hell:

What do you think about this understanding of "sin", commonly believed to be the ticket to hell?

God, all-loving and totally centered in divine bliss, is offended for us not by us. If we need to speak about "God" and "sin" in human terms we might better say that God's reaction to sin is one of anguish not anger. God knows our sins hurt us and others in the family of God, commonly referred to as the human race. Sin makes us less oriented to our better selves, to other family members and to God. But God does not become less oriented to "sinners". God's love is beyond such pettiness. God does not return sin with sin. "Offense against God" may not be the best way of describing what is commonly called "sin."

If some sinners seem to prosper in sin while others are crushed by prospering sinners it is not up to us to determine how God deals with those injustices in the next life. It is time to let go of our hell stories. Our faith should assure us that God knows how to sort things out in a more godly way.

Our so-called "mortal sins" are not rejections of God's love – not even missing mass on Sunday, practicing birth control, divorcing and remarrying without an annulment, same sex marriages, doubting church doctrines. Not one of these or all of them taken together can be taken as saying "I don't love God" or "I don't even want God to love me." They are what they are, hard choices and sometimes even harmful choices, nothing more, nothing less.

Some thought-provoking questions:

1. Ask your clergyman:

If there is no hell does that mean there are no devils? What would be the point? What would be their incentive?

If there is no hell is there any special punishment for the countless clergy who preached on hell and added unnecessary misery to the dying days of countless millions?

If the Pope and Billy Graham say we should not take "hellfire" literally why should we take "eternal" literally? Surely if "fire" is only a metaphor so then is "eternal".

Is the traditional teaching on going to hell kosher? Hellworthy sins of all sizes and shapes are thrown at us except the sin featured in Jesus' last parable on hell, the sin of not treating the least as if they were Jesus?

Is it not true that a Christian might be easily led to believe that in his last parable Jesus said: "Whatever you do to the Lords you do unto me: When I was angry you did not fear me. When I was in full regalia you did not revere me. When I was pontificating you did not obey me. Depart from me ye accursed into the everlasting fires."

Is it appropriate for Christianity to feature hell for about 2000 years and then simply say "fuhgheddaboutit"?

2. Ask yourself:

Did Jesus make his references to hell as the divine son of God or the Jewish son of Mary?

If there is no hell as advertised is there a heaven as advertised? If we are not bad enough for hell why believe we are good enough for heaven?

A personal crisis:

It was one thing to rely on research, careful preparation, and the sometimes muted but always present advantage that goes with being the teacher and standing at the lectern. It was one thing to use this advantage to challenge the images of God and Son as almighty presences highlighted by the threat of eternal pain and the promise of eternal joy.

But it was quite something else to hold that challenge in my heart during Sunday worship. The architecture, the rituals, the readings, the sermons, the believers gathered with me favored and even demanded a reverence for God and Son as being most godly in their almighty powers. No sermons I heard in church sounded like my lectures. Not one priest ever put the divinity of Jesus or the threat of hell on the church windowsill. The subtext at Sunday worship was this:

We are here to worship and rely on God as the Father Almighty or pay the almighty consequences.

Yes, my friends, I lectured one way and worshiped another. And then, after a few years of lecturing this contradiction finally caught up with me. I had a remarkable religious experience during Sunday Mass.

11. ONE SUNDAY AT MASS -
(May, 1985)

I could not pray to God as 'Almighty'

It happened suddenly, without warning.

I stood in silence as the congregation began the creed.

I was not bored, lazy, or distracted.

I was not untouched by the faith of those around me.

I was not unaware of the graces being received.

I was not angry with God.

I had not lost my faith in God.

I was silent because the opening words of the creed stuck in my throat. And it was about time I might add. I had not experienced God as an almighty presence in my life on the road. If not while trying to live with and work for the poor as Jesus did, then when should I experience God as an almighty presence? My life on the road rudely awakened me.

I could not bring myself to address God as "the Almighty" – even after having done so for thousands of Sundays, both in the pew as a layman and at the altar as a priest.

This was no small matter.

I was at war with the heart of my Tradition.

I was as stunned in my silence as you may be in reading about it. I had prayed to God as almighty since I was a child. And I did quite well doing so, along with the countless others who gladly and gracefully relate to God as Father Almighty, as instructed by Scripture and Tradition.

And yet, here I stood, in church, unable to honor God as an almighty fatherly presence among us, or even an almighty motherly presence for that matter.

Why did the words "Father Almighty" stick in my throat?

Was Satan seducing me? That could not be it. I do not believe in a devil that makes me do bad things. I take full responsibility for my behavior. In any case, such a late-in-life seduction of a long-time religious guy like me could suggest that Satan, if there is a Satan, is mightier than God almighty.

Was senility setting in? I don't think so. I seemed to be of sound mind and body. I was still lecturing and grading exams, shopping and cooking, laughing and crying at appropriate times. My wife was not afraid to leave me home alone.

Was it possible that my silence at the Creed was not a problem? Could my silence be a grace rather than a disgrace? Could it be the grace of finally putting aside the metaphor of God as "all-mighty" so that I might more fully embrace the metaphor of God as "all-mystery"? Could it be that this is the only way I could learn to love "the mystery"? Could it be that in my life of faith God as mystery was finally beginning to trump God as almighty?

But wait, you may say. From day one, nature's power to terrorize and to bless had hardwired "almighty" into humanity's image of God. Humanity has always feared God's power to punish us and trusted in God's power to save us. God is God because of his Almighty Power. To go against that belief would mean going against humanity's experience of God.

Hold on, I reply. Thanks to Science men have walked on the moon. We no longer worship the sun and moon as divine beings. Thanks to Science the book of Genesis is now read as sacred stories not as scientific facts. Many believers do not believe that the universe began not too long ago with God saying let there be this and let there be that.

Thanks to the sciences of archeology and biblical studies many believers do not take the book of Exodus literally. God did not kill Egyptian babies. There was no parting of the Red Sea. A pillar of fire did not lead twelve tribes through the desert. There was no golden calf, no bread from heaven.

Thanks to our experience of God's presence in the history of the modern world we have good reason to say that it is more mysterious than mighty. God seems to be mighty shy about using almighty power on planet earth – too shy even to send a few plagues Hitler's way, even though Hitler was a thousand times harder on the Jews than any Pharaoh. One can rightly and piously say that God's presence on planet earth is a matter of faith. And, thanks to God's good sense, it is not a faith proven by miracles or backed by facts.

Not so fast, you may say. You cannot discount the Genesis and Exodus teaching so easily. The Genesis account of creation may only be a story, but it is an inspired story with a lesson: God brought us into this world and God can just as easily take us out. That is lesson number one of the bible. One cannot be a devout bible reader and then hesitate to address God as "almighty". The bible stories make one thing perfectly clear:

God is mighty, we are needy. God is the solution, we are the problem.

Hold on, I reply. Bible readers tend to forget that the bible stories and their lessons were shaped when believers could not imagine God as being anything but an "almighty presence". In biblical times, when it rained it was because God opened the flood-gates of heaven. When it did not rain it was because God kept those Gates closed. Each day and night God sent or held back the rain. If a plague was needed to get a job done God did what a God had to do. God had both hands on the wheel of the universe, with one foot on the throttle and the other on the brakes. Nature and history were simply God's obedient servants, nothing but putty in his hands.

The biblical stories of God as the Almighty are inspired attempts to describe how in primitive times God was believed to be present on this planet. But how God is truly present on planet earth is a mystery and will always be one, even if a hundred bibles were written under the inspiration of God. Inspiration is a miracle of grace not a grace that works miracles. A miracle of inspiration would be a Genesis story that gave an account similar to that of Darwin. To take the Genesis story as an explanation of how God goes about being God almighty would be as wrong as wrong could be.

There is a big difference between a presence that takes billions of years and one that takes six days to get the job done. One is the presence of a humble God saying "I left no fingerprints, no footprints, as few clues as possible - I am still a mystery". The other is a show-off presence that boasts "I'm God Almighty, I'm running this show, and you better believe it."

There is a big difference between the hand that shapes two adults from the dust of the earth and one that takes billions of years to get the job done. In one God is saying "You're putty in my almighty hands". In the other we are co-creators of the incarnation of divine life.

Wrong! you may say. Enough with the fancy talk. The mystery of God is simply this: How can one person make a world, destroy a world, save sinners, and, above all, keep sinners suffering forever – and ever? Divine mystery is but the flip side of divine might.

So you say, and so say most believers! No wonder a noted historian soundly criticized Christianity for confusing mystery with might: "The primitive Christians perpetually trod on mystic ground and their minds were exercised by the habits of believing the most extraordinary events."

The extraordinary events believed are usually those of power, beginning with the story of God making the world in a creative instant and destroying what he created in an apocalyptic fury.

For most believers only an almighty earthling could be revered as an incarnation of God Almighty. It made sense for the ancient Romans to hail Caesar as an incarnation of divine might. He carved out an empire with the sword. But it makes no sense to hail the Nazarene as an incarnation of divine might. He was no Moses, David, Caesar, or Mohammed. He came to bury the sword not to brandish it in battle.

Revering Jesus as an incarnation of divine might made no sense until there were stories about him defeating Satan, opening heaven and satisfying the wrath of God. Without those stories there would be no belief in the Nazarene as the incarnation of a God believed to be an almighty presence on planet earth. That God is always the hammer, never ever the nail.

Some thought-provoking observations:

1. Clearly, God is determined to be silent, to be unseen, to be a presence that is barely traceable - to be the exact opposite of an almighty presence.

2. Why this is so is not for me to say. Perhaps it is because an almighty presence would kick the stuffing out of our faith.

3. If God hardly ever, if ever, shows an almighty presence, though it is so often requested by so many, and if "almighty" means what it usually means, it seems childish to honor God as Father Almighty. "Father" is O.K. as a metaphor but "Almighty" is clearly the wrong metaphor for characterizing God's presence among us.

4. Saying to yourself: "God help me" is an emotional expression, one much like telling someone to "Go to hell." Both frequently used expressions should help remind us that God is not at our beck and call as "the Almighty".

5. If we keep insisting that God is an almighty presence I would not be surprised if some day believers and unbelievers alike would be tempted to chant: "Poor God is dead. He was almighty but he never showed it."

6. It would be well to consider the following:

Anything is possible with God – even being present on earth as an all loving rather than an all mighty presence.

No doubt, God is "Almighty" in some mysterious way. But if God has decided not to flaunt divine might then why should we? God hides divine might yet we highlight it? Do we know better than God as to how God should go about being godly?

Even in the bible stories God's mighty deeds seem to be mighty more in theory than in practice: the "garden of paradise" plan failed; the "land of milk and honey" plan is a bloody mess; the "kingdom of God on earth" plan is in danger of a nuclear meltdown. Spiritual bean counters could make the case that down through the ages Satan seems to be even mightier than God.

In considering the image of God as being in charge of the universe I am reminded of a Yiddish saying: "If God lived on earth people would break his windows."

Some thought-provoking suppositions:

Suppose it is the goal of God to establish perfect love rather than perfect order in his kingdom on earth. The goal of perfect order would demand an all controlling presence. But the goal of perfect love would require the exact opposite. Anyone who knows anything about love knows this.

Suppose the bible stories about God say more about us than about God. After all, since we worship power we are primed to expect that a God who talks the talk and walks the walk of almighty power is the greatest of all possible blessings. God has yet to take the bait of humanity's all too human expectations.

Suppose God is playing the mystery card and we are trumping it with the almighty card. It may be that my silence during the creed is a grace, not a disgrace.

A disturbing dilemma:

I was making headway teaching in the classroom and at worship in church. But this had little effect on my daily life of prayer. It seemed that I had inherited from my tradition and from most of the human race a prayer life I could not live without. I prayed as if God would use his almighty power to help me. Get me this job. Get me out of this mess. Cure that cancer. Lift this burden. Don't let so-and-so be elected president. Almost always to little avail.

Since Day One it was assumed that begging for help from the almighty powers above was the only way to get help. It was assumed that we would be lost without our pitiful pleading hands and God's almighty helping hand.

It is no wonder that my classroom lectures and my silence during the creed had little effect on my daily life of prayer. I continued to beg for help from the Almighty as much as the next guy – that is until I was blessed with another surprising and life-changing religious experience.

The biggest surprise of all was that it took place during a summer vacation.

12. THE VACATION INCIDENT - (June, 1993)

A radical new experience of prayer

Before I tell you about this experience I must tell you why I worried so much about prayer, about talking to God.

I was taught that God is always listening. For some reason I began to worry that God might be upset because I talk much, much, much less with 'him' than I do with anyone else: "Hey, I'm God, I'm listening. How come you give me less than an hour a day? What am I, chopped liver?" That could very well be God's attitude if God is more "touchy" about keeping in touch than I care to admit.

Worse yet, when I talk to God I speak more with my lips than from the heart, and of my needs more than my love. Is God offended that so many of my prayers are not heartfelt expressions of love? I surely hope not. But what if God loves only lovers? Do my prayers work against me? Is it a waste of time to pray unless I can pray in the proper spirit? Genesis chapter four has a story about praying in the proper spirit. The smoke from Abel's sacrifice went up to God but the smoke from Cain's did not. Cain burnt his easily spared crops while Abel burnt the best of his first-born animals. Cain was praying on the cheap. Am I praying on the cheap? Does my smoke go up to God?

I also worried about praying for forgiveness. Jesus taught us to ask God to forgive us only as we forgive those who trespass against us. What a bummer! That sounds too much like a "pre-forgiveness agreement" – one that puts me at a serious disadvantage. If God forgives only as I forgive, then I am in trouble – and so are you. Looking at asking for forgiveness from the perspective of The Lord's prayer can be mighty unnerving.

The Lord's Prayer is even more unnerving when compared to the story of the Ten Commandments. God and Son do not seem to be on the same page when it comes to forgiving. In the commandment story God vows to punish the children of those who offended him, "down to the third and fourth generations…" Of course, he's God, and can do what he pleases. But can we be expected to be more forgiving than God?

I worried about the unforgiving attitude of Christianity. Until recently Christians did not even bother to fake forgiveness of "the Jews" whom they had branded as "Christ killers". For almost 2,000 years the Christian prayer has been: "Father, forgive us as we do not forgive the Jews."

I had another problem with prayer. What about praying for bread? Jesus taught us to ask the Father for our daily bread. Twice the story is told that Jesus made that prayer come true, miraculously feeding the multitude with loaves and fishes. In college I read Aldous Huxley's take on the miracle of the loaves and fishes. He claimed that Jesus did not miraculously multiply the loaves. By the power of his personality and preaching he moved those who had bread to share it with those who had failed to bring bread in their haste to hear and see Jesus. I was upset at the time. Huxley claimed that Jesus merely aroused a kind and generous sharing – as could any decent preacher. I told my spiritual director of Huxley's interpretation. He calmed me down by saying: "How the hell does Huxley know what happened?" But then he added: "It's not a bad interpretation, Jim. It encourages people to share their bread generously rather than expect God to do the feeding." That response made sense to me.

But if Jesus did not miraculously feed the people then what does that one day in the life of Jesus tell us? Did it testify that the wretched, the poor and the huddled masses will be fed by human generosity not divine intervention? What does the story of miracles down through the centuries tell us about God? Hoping for divine intervention is like hoping to win the lottery. In prayer, however, it is not the odds working against us but God's decision to use divine might mighty sparingly, if at all. How often does God use his almighty power to cure a cancer, rattle a rapist, control a child molester, or halt a holocaust? Why did God not even lift a finger in the plot to assassinate Hitler? Why do we pray to God as almighty if the almighty seldom, if ever, uses his "almightiness" to intervene in an almighty way? In this kind of prayer as in the lottery it is wise to keep our expectations low.

I lived with my questions and worries about bidding for help for quite some time. You may think I was just a worry wart. But that's the kind of guy I am. I am not the kind of guy who finds peace in the claim that prayer worries vanish once you accept Jesus as your personal Savior. I am too much a Roman Catholic for that. Besides, I would worry about family and friends who do not accept Jesus as their personal Savior – along with most of the human race. Becoming an Evangelical Protestant was not my way out of worrying about prayer. My way out was a grace of another color – a radically new experience of prayer.

The Grace of a Seven Word Sentence:
"Bidden or not bidden, God is present"

It was the summer of 1993. I was on vacation in England. I was being pleasured by an ancient church – by its art, architecture and history. I was in a house of God but God was not on my mind. I was in this church as a tourist. I almost missed seeing the "bidden or not" text cited above. It was finely chiseled over an archway, barely visible - as if those in charge were uncertain as to whether or not it belonged in a Christian Church. I read it as a hesitant whisper not a bold proclamation. But its seven words stopped me in my tourist tracks. Suddenly, God was on my mind. Or, to be more precise, a God-scene took shape in my imagination – the God-spot of the mind.

Setting: East of Eden, the day after the troubles.

God is laughing at Adam and Eve, learning
how to kneel, somewhat clumsily, as if they
were Protestants at a Catholic wedding.

God: "Now what? What's this all about? What's going
on here?"

Adam: "We are trying to find the body position
best suited for begging. We are trying to
learn how to bid for your help. Now that
we are outside the garden we will need
plenty of help.

God: "Such nonsense! You are still my images.
You still have dominion over the earth.
Begging suits neither you nor me. Your
mission, if you care to accept it, is to
make planet earth the best it can be."

Eve: "Is that why we had to leave the Garden?"

God: "Of course, why else? Eating from that
tree was a happy mistake. It helped me let
you go out on your own. Just remember:
Bidden or not bidden I am always present.
But I will be present as a companion not as

a caretaker. I will hold your hand. Rarely,
will I lift a finger in a godly way. You
were created as my images. You must live
up to my great expectations. Get up off
your knees. No begging, please. Bidden or
not I will always be by your side.
That's my plan and I'm sticking to it."

Meanwhile, in the real world, I am standing transfixed,
mouth open, jaw dropped, and heart beating rapidly. Yes, yes,
yes, yes, I am saying to myself – much like an excited child and
yet with a thrill that usually comes only with sexual intimacy.
At that moment I began experiencing God as a simple flat-out
presence, with no "ifs" or "buts". God is godly in an ungodly
casual and unassuming way.

Slowly, and yet quickly, a series of questions tempered my
euphoria, calmed me down. How could all of humanity be so
wrong about God? Since Day One of the human race it was
assumed that divine beings are bossy, demanding, and very
uppity about bidding properly. Long before the bible, "bidding"
was presumed to be what the Gods and Goddesses demanded

and highly prized. The overarching theme of religion has been "Beg properly and you may get some help. Our biblical God fit in with this tradition. Indeed, he turned "bidding properly" into a fine art.

This "bidden quote" and my wild imagination do not stand up well against humanity's experience of God, the portrait of God in the bible, nor even my own experience of prayer. Begging while on my knees seemed to work well for me, though never in a dramatic way – nothing like prayer restoring my knees after a knee-destroying accident.

How could this quote be engraved on the wall of a Christian church? Where was my imagination taking me? Dare I imagine God as an equal opportunity companion to sinner and saint alike, to those who pray and those who do not, to those who worship and those who do not? What kind of God is equally present to all whether bidden or not. Sheer nonsense! I may as well call God a bleeding-heart liberal.

I was stunned at my audacity. Then I realized I was in an Anglican Church, a church derided by some for its vague and even laughably tolerant standards of faith. I've turned God into some sort of Anglican, I thought. I sat down. I tried to pull myself together. I was entertaining an ungodly portrait of God.

Still, I could not deny the powerful impact triggered by this simple seven word sentence. Its assurance of a casual and unassuming "ungodly" presence held my imagination captive. Try as I might I could not dismiss this image of God. At first I told myself that perhaps God is present in such a quiet and non-threatening way only with old people like me. Maybe he eases up on us because we are so near the green pastures, because we need a shepherd more than a lord. Yes, that had to be it. What I had experienced was very personal. I should keep it to myself. It would not be prudent to share this with anyone. It would be irresponsible to write about it as if it were a theology of prayer. Such a theology would make mince meat out of the image of God shared by humanity since Day One.

I kept reminding myself – say nothing to no one. If this experience of God helps you get through the last chapter of your life so much the better. Do not interpret this bidden quote as if you were a theologian. You are a theologian by training but not a practicing theologian. You preferred "passion or perish" over "publish or perish". That was your choice. Stay away from the public forum. And that's what I did.

But in my heart and soul, in my mind and my spirit, in whatever it is that makes me tick as a spiritual being that seven word sentence had its way with me. I knew that my experience in that church was something more than that of a sentimental old man flirting with senility and death. I came to believe that one of my rudest awakenings was this new-found awareness that God is godly in the most ungodly way. This soft and subtle presence of God, constant companion to all, was almost too good to believe. But I did believe.

Most of all, I felt blessed in being able to approach the so called golden years (I was 63 years old) abiding in God as present, whether bidden or not bidden. "Golden" would be for me more than a trite cover for being old. Golden for me meant that I was becoming as hopeful as Gempel the Fool, a fictional character whose words were becoming my words:

"When the time comes I will go joyfully.
Whatever may be there, it will be real,
without complication, without ridicule,
without deception. God be praised."

It was in this thoroughly hopeful and relaxed mood that my religious imagination kicked into high gear, as you will see in the next chapter.

13. SURPRISED BY MY VIVID IMAGINATION - (Late 1990's)

A short story and a tall tale

As surprised as I was by the vacation incident I was even more surprised when I came across the following short story:

"Three Jews were boasting of their rabbis, and one said, 'My rabbi's faith is so great and he fears the Lord so much that he trembles day and night, and he has to be belted into his bed with straps so that he doesn't fall out.'

The second said, 'Yes, you have a marvelous rabbi, But he really can't be compared to my rabbi. Mine is so holy and so just that he makes God tremble. God is afraid of displeasing him. And if the world has not been going so well lately, you can figure it out for yourselves. God is trembling.'

The third Jew said, 'Your rabbis are both
great men. No doubt about it. But my rabbi
passed through both stages. For a long time he
trembled, too, and in the second stage,
he made God tremble. But then he thought
it over very carefully and finally he said to God,
'Look – why should we both tremble?'"

("Great Jewish Short Stories" – Saul Bellow, ed.)

This story made me chuckle. But it did more than that. It stoked up my vivid imagination. The story allowed me to imagine that God could tremble. Such is the power of the good story teller.

As you know, the Jews are great story tellers. Their skill in telling bible stories still holds many in awe. Their stories in texts other than the bible are also inspiring. Like the one just cited, they can be humorous too. But this humor is not for our entertainment.

Picturing God as trembling is no joke. It is a radical commentary on the mystery of God. The bible portrays God as tremble-maker, never as trembling. The bible does portray God as being emotional. But his emotions are those of an all-powerful God. He shows wrath against sinners. He is jealous of other gods. He even regrets having created humanity. Wrath and jealousy go well with power. So does regret – when it is followed by a ruthless punishment. But trembling is an emotion unworthy of almighty God. The almighty do not tremble.

I embrace this story of God trembling. Trembling is an emotion that fits well my sense of God as all-loving. I am sick and tired of living with stories and beliefs that favor God as all-powerful. I am sick and tired of worrying about what God will do when we behave badly. I am tired of the tiresome tradition that I am made holy by divine threats. I've had it with the tradition that the way to God requires four virtues: faith, hope, love – and worry. My teachers did not have to include worry on their official list of virtues since worry was not a virtue I needed to cultivate. Worry flourished in my fear that "sin" offends God, in my expectation that God reacts to it "fist first". My worries and expectations were fed by my vision of God as a tremble-maker.

In immersing myself in the Yiddish story of a God who worries about offending us and a God who trembles, my imagination kicked in. I began to imagine God saying to himself:

"Creation was my idea, my plan. The mess is mainly my mess. The tension between the Old Revelation and New Revelation is my mess. The tragedy of a chosen people becoming accursed through the centuries is my mess. The predominance of fear over love among my believers is my mess. The love of certitude over mystery among my teachers is my mess."

Reading news accounts about massive floods I can easily imagine God trembling after flooding the world:

"Did I overdo it? Did I act like a feckless thug? Were my motives well-grounded? Did I read all human hearts fairly? Was every human heart truly inclined to do evil? Should I have saved the animals?"

I am not so simple minded as to imagine God could and should tremble as I have just described. Nor am I so simple minded as to believe God could and should become so enraged and punitive that he would flood a world. But I ask myself, would God be offended if in preaching, teaching or writing about the tale of the flood I added the detail of God trembling? I think not. Taking such liberties was a common practice among the Jews who gave us these stories. I am also encouraged by the anti-tremble liberties that Rabbi Jesus takes in his tall tales about the Good Shepherd and the Prodigal son. So it was in good faith that I made up this story about God:

My Tall Tale about God Repenting
God's Agony in the Garden of Eden

Time: Thousands of years after Eden was closed.
(a thousand years are as a day in God's eyes)

Scene: God sitting with an angel, another angel still
guarding the gate to the garden. God is beating
his breast, saying "mea culpa, mea culpa, mea
maxima culpa" (my fault, my fault, my most grievous
fault). He is repeating over and over the words of
a future poet: "How seamless seemed love, and then
came the troubles."

God: In a fit of rage

      I filled the world with water.

      I did not even shed a furtive tear.

      My Bad!

      In an act of fear I scattered humanity,

      And took away its common language.

      Now everyone who spoke differently

      was no longer trusted.

      War was invented and taught to the children.

      Cities were fortified. My Bad!

      In a stubborn mood I destroyed Sodom.

      Abraham pushed me to lower the price of mercy,

      as if we were merchants in the market-place.

      I did not even spare the women and children.

      They were in no way involved in the gang rapes.

      My Shame!

      In a temper tantrum I almost killed Moses.

      His wife did not want their baby circumcised.

      "Too painful" she complained.

He allowed his wife to complain.

To complain against my holy will!

I almost killed Moses for that.

Moses was my main man in my main plan.

My stupidity!

In a most ungodly moment,

after the golden calf incident,

I condemned those who escaped Egypt

to wander for forty years in the desert:

This meant that none of them would enter the

promised land. Since there was no heaven,

Moses and his exodus people got nothing in return

for their faith.

My cruelty!

In my most ungodly moment I made my worst

mistake. I believed, as do humans, that justice

can be served only by meeting evil with evil,

responding to violence with violence, answering

sin with sin. Can you believe it?

No cruelty was too excessive.

My blasphemy!

Angel: What happened? Why do you think you
behaved so badly?

God: In the beginning I behaved as you would
expect - as Mr. Generosity, Mr. Congeniality.
I want to make one thing perfectly clear.
I did not expel Adam and Eve from the Garden.
I did not send a serpent to tempt them.
Why would I even think of testing their love?
And why so quickly? Besides, if I had sent a
talking serpent I would have said so. I never
made such a claim. The talking serpent was
a tall tale told by the story teller.
It helped him explain evil in paradise.
Another tall tale, sillier than a talking serpent,
is that of women as inferior to men.
The story teller claims I condemned all
women to be dumb enough to crave a man
even though men would boss them around
and make them pregnant. And, to add insult

to injury I supposedly caused birthing
to be painful. Such nonsense!

This is what really happened.
Adam, Eve and I were a happy threesome.
We delighted walking arm in arm
in the evening breeze of the garden.
One evening, walking by a very unusual tree,
I gave them my opinion, not a command. We
were lovers. We didn't give or take commands.
Our relationship was one of intimacy, not
one of submission.

They thought eating from that tree,
The tree of knowledge of good and evil,
would help them be more like me.
They did not realize that once they knew about
evil they could not stay in the garden
of "no evil". They made a mistake. They did
not commit a sin. They knew they had to leave
and accepted it without question. I knew
they would since they were images of me.

Believe me! No sin was involved. I hugged
a frightened Adam and put an arm around a
a saddened Eve. I assured them that outside
the garden they would not have to beg for help.

But the separation was heartbreaking for us.
We sensed that once separated things would
go badly between us. We felt that the three
of us would change for the worse. And so it did.
Their downhill slide was heartbreaking. But I
matched it step for step – as I have already
confessed.

They began to fear me as all-powerful and
I played into that fear. I now thought in
terms of commands not opinions. I was not
good at handling disobedience.
I almost always went at it fist first.
I tremble at my behavior after our separation.

Some day some will claim that I had
my son crucified. I did no such thing.

Given my reputation the claim is understandable.

My son will tremble in the garden of Gethsemane.

He will have learned from his mother and his rabbis

the Torah stories about me as a tremble-maker.

He will come to believe that his cruel death

might even be my will.

My son will tremble in the garden of Gethsemane.

I tremble in my agony in the Garden of Eden.

I already hear his pleading prayer in the

garden and his Godforsaken prayer on the cross.

Believe me! God can and does tremble."

The Yiddish story ends with "Why should we both tremble?"
My story closes with "God can and does tremble."
If it were not for the Gospel story of a trembling Jesus on the
cross I would not dare to tell my story of a trembling God. To
the extent that Jesus reveals God he reveals that God can be a
powerless presence among us and can tremble with us. What a
story: Rabbi Jesus and his Hebrew speaking Father, both

trembling. Why not? If we are allowed to image God as a terrorist why not imagine God as a trembler? Taken literally, both images are equally nonsense.

Yes indeed, I thought, my vivid imagination is going to give me much to think about. I must give more and more time to pondering. That turned out to be only too true. When I retired it was pondering, not research, that provided me the stuff this book is made of.

I pondered as a friend talking to friends not as a scholar contributing to his discipline. But I could not help pondering as one who had studied theology, preached theology and taught theology.

At first I tried to put together a dumbed-down theology book. My working title was "Rude Awakenings about God and Son." But a series of rejections to some sample chapters convinced me there was no market for my book. I was told that publishers would shy away from it because it fell into a grey area between "theology" and "memoir". It was neither fish nor fowl. With the encouragement of a literary agent who showed interest in the two chapters I sent him I used what I thought was a book as a notebook for a manuscript that was more memoir than theology. At each rewrite the manuscript became more and more memoir – a reflection on my journey into the heart of spiritual transformation.

14. AT HOME PONDERING -
(2000- 2008)

When I retired I did the cooking and food shopping since my wife was still working as a social worker in the Baltimore Public School System. But this was a welcome distraction from the intense time spent pondering. Pondering time became the great gray grace of my life. I came close to drooling over the pondering time I now had.

Pondering not research filled my notebooks and the scraps of paper on my desk, all over the house, stuffed in my pockets and in the pocket of the car door. Sometimes I pondered for hours and then would throw away my notes. Sometimes a few minutes would give me precious pages. Anything could trigger my going into a deep pondering freeze. But if I were to tag one event as the inauguration of serious pre-book pondering it would have to be my mother's funeral. She died the year I retired. My retirement pondering began as that of a bereaved son not a probing theologian. What I began to put on paper were more meditations than theological investigations.

My Mother Mary:

In her last years my mom told me she felt like she was living in the vestibule between this world and the next. She was leaving this world but had not left. Worse yet, she was afraid to die. I reminded her of the old saying: "Everyone wants to get to heaven but no one wants to die to get there." She did not smile nor did I. I knew why there was no joy in the hours of her dying. She was afraid to enter the world of the almighty white Guy with a beard. Her Pope insisted that the sin of birth control would send her straight to hell. She believed she had done the right thing in controlling the number of children she had.

My mother had a right to be afraid. Her church served a strong brew every Sunday, served it at the insistence of Popes and Patriarchs. This strong drink brought us all to our feet crying out "I believe" not "It seems to me." "It seems to me" was the best my mother could say about birth control.

Was I wrong in assuring my mother she had nothing to worry about – as I did from time to time as life began to slip away from her?

My patron Saint thought so. He blind-sided me as I was preparing for my mom's funeral mass. He had been going at me since the day I stood in Church and said "it seems to me" that I should not pray to God as Father Almighty:

James. I'm your patron saint. I'm going to say this and I'm going to say it only once. God does not take kindly to those who wallow in doubt. It seems to me is messing with the Pope, the Vicar of Christ. Read my lips:

"...the one who doubts is like the wave of the sea,

driven and tossed by the wind; for the doubter,

being double-minded and unstable in every way,

must not expect to receive anything from the Lord."

(James: 1: 6-8)

James my boy, you are about to bury your mother. You better start reflecting on the long-revered hymn sung at funeral masses, the "Dies Irae" (The Day of Wrath).

You have heard it often enough in your life. Surely you remember it well enough to imagine God singing along with the church choir, in a deep, disturbing, divine voice:

'That day of wrath, that dreadful day...

What terror then to us shall fall

when lo, the Judge's steps appall,

about to weigh the deeds of all...

The book is opened, that the dead

may hear their doom from what is read,

the record of our conscience dread..."

But, thanks to my mother's granddaughters and liturgical changes introduced in the Second Vatican Council the hymns sung at her funeral were nothing like the "Dies Irae". The hymns sung highlighted God as lover and friend, not as an avenging judge. At her funeral we sang:

"Amazing Grace"

"Be not Afraid"

"On Eagle's Wings"

"Let there be peace on earth"

"The Lord is my Shepherd."

These hymns are more appropriate for a "Welcome Home, Mary" rather than "The Court is now in session". They are more soothing than frightening. Arriving home on eagle's wings, finding a shepherd there instead of a judge, having no fears, being only concerned about peace on earth – all this sounds more like a day of fun rather than a day of fury. These hymns stirred up great expectations. While singing them I could imagine my mom laughing and joking with Jimmy Durante and Mrs. Kalabash.

Yes, my friends, the ritual surrender of the "Dies Irae" to hymns of hope and joy was truly an amazing grace. In terms of graces this is as good as it gets. Going from here to eternity is crunch time. Music can ease the crunch for those left behind. The "Dies Irae" worked well as long as it did only because the music was classic and the words were in Latin. But who today wants to send their loved ones to parts unknown with a song of dread, wrath, terror and doom – with the added torment of a judge whose steps are appalling and who insists on the weighing of our deeds, birth control included?

The teaching that we first meet God as "the Judge" rather than as "our Father" is as bewildering as it is frightening. Could not God as a loving Father work out the good and the bad we have done and do it like the father of the prodigal son? Could we answer that question without bringing up guys like Hitler?

I have always feared meeting God in a courtroom setting. I dreaded this even more so after having been on trial. The courtroom was as intimidating as a room can be. The prosecutors have the home court advantage. The judge, without a word, is saying don't even think of messing with me. His black robes and highly placed take-charge chair are ominous. The man in black has the look and smell of power.

The judge did not see me as Jim La Croce. He saw only the accused, the defendant, the law-breaker, escorted by guards from a locked jail. Legally I was innocent until proven guilty. Emotionally, I was a prisoner until proven innocent. There were restrictions to what I could say and do on my behalf.

I understand the need for courtroom procedures. I do not favor the courtroom as a metaphor for our meeting up with God on planet heaven.

By the grace of liturgical reforms, and my mom's granddaughters, the songs I heard at my mom's funeral were more fitting for meeting God as a lover than a fearsome judge. I do believe I am not out of line in imagining a scenario even more comforting than mom meeting Jimmy Durante:

God has the face of a loving parent, a beloved friend, an intimate lover – something along those lines. God is bending over my mother, bending over backwards, showing her all the understanding a divine lover can show. God is evidently partial, biased and markedly fond of her, perhaps even 'madly in love' with her. And yet, I can imagine mom still has birth control on her mind. This is when my vivid imagination gets a boost from a poet. I imagine God being calm and casual about her fears...

"...settling a pillow or throwing off a shawl,

and turning toward the window, should say

'That is not it at all,

That is not what I meant at all.'"

(T.S.Eliot, "The Love Song of J. Alfred Prufrock.")

Jesus' Mother Mary:

The child of a father who goes by the book obeys his father but his heart belongs to his mother. Before punishments she intervenes. After them she hugs. That is why my heart belonged to Mary not to the Father Almighty. It was my greatest hope that if the story of God hardening Pharaoh's heart had any lesson for me it was that Mary could soften God's heart. Was I ever in for a surprise. Let me tell you about it.

•••

The Night Visitor:

In one wild and crazy dream Mary entered the God-spot of my mind, the imagination, and put the pedal to the metal:

Jim, you're an idiot!

Why are you asking me to soften God's heart? That is so stupid. God's heart was womb-softened over two thousand years ago.

Why do you fear God as "the almighty"? Why in God's name do you think God arrived on planet earth as "all-needy" rather than as "all mighty"?

I repeat what I just said, and no one has the right to say it more than me. In the fullness of time God came to planet earth as an all-needy presence not an all-mighty presence. In my womb this incarnation of God lived only by the beat of my heart. If that is not a down to earth hard core revelation of God as present among us as "all-needy" rather than as "all-mighty" I don't know what is.

From womb, to breast, to crib, to lap, to infancy years I gave life to an incarnation of God. I was God to that incarnation. While pregnant that incarnation lived in me, through me and by me. In those blessed days you could say that I was God to God. I am not boasting about myself. Who needs that? I'm boasting about God. If I am not proof positive that in becoming flesh God sent planet earth a "love me" invitation I don't know what is. What more could God do to put an end to the frightening stories of his almighty presence on planet earth? Do you think this incarnation as an infant was just a slide-show for your Christmas celebration – a little treat for the children? No way! God became a diapered deity for grown-ups. His poo and pee had as much to do with his incarnation as his blood.

My giving flesh to Jesus was as unlike God giving flesh to Adam as fact is unlike fiction, as powering down is unlike powering up. My son was not sent as the "Anti-Adam". There was no Adam, no cosmic fall from grace, no need for humanity to be born again, no irreversible state of corruption. On planet earth there is only laziness, lust in all shapes and forms (some more violent and greedy than others) and a lack of leadership. My son fought all of these as a powered-down son of God before being nailed prematurely. His premature death was more tragic than magic. It did not save the world from sin and error, as history has made evident.

Yes, we are all born with weaknesses and inclinations, born as imperfect creatures, born into a world seeking whom it may devour. But this endears us to God. It does not alienate us. What kind of Father would that be? You tell me!

Jim! Everyone is born as beloved by God. The story of my being conceived without sin is a way of revealing everyone is so conceived. I repeat! There was no Adam. There was no original sin. The feast of my immaculate conception is the feast of your immaculate conception. You do well to take pride in being ordained a priest on the hundredth anniversary of the church's official declaration that I was conceived without original sin. You were ordained on the feast celebrating your immaculate conception.

Get real, Jim. God went all the way in this fleshy and messy incarnation. You know what going all the way means don't you? It is the love of intimates not of infants. Do you think God is asking only for your child-like love, a love kept alive by threats and promises? Get real, Jim.

Jim! Are you incapable of imagining a God whose love went all the way, whose love is a weapon of mass seduction? I hope not. I hope you and your fellow believers have not become children of a lesser God.

(I thought Mary had said her piece. But no, she had to get in her parting shot):

Jim! God's need for me was only a foreshadowing of God's need for you. Without you there can be no kingdom of God on earth. You know how much that kingdom means to God and son. You do remember the Lord's Prayer don't you? If God and Son could have made the kingdom come on their own don't you think it would be done by now? Get real, Jim. God needs you more than you need God.

....

What could I say? For me the incarnation is only a religious experience. For Mary it was a flesh and blood experience. How can Protestants make light of my devotion to Mary? That Jesus began his life in her womb, suckled at her breast, was fondled, fed, kissed and hugged by her makes her a key player in the revelation that life and love between God and us are irretrievably enmeshed. Mary's womb, breast, lap, arms and eyes are the great Amen to God's command to Israel: "Hear, O Israel… You shall love the Lord your God with all your heart, and with all your soul, and with all your mind, and with all your strength."(Deuteronomy 6: 4-6).

If those words and that womb mean anything then my love of God should be a heart-throbbing not a knee-bending love. I should consider it a failure if there is so little of this kind of love in me when I die that God would have to wave a magic wand over my heart to make my love heaven-worthy.

Some Protestants claim there is such a wand. It is the blood of Christ. It makes God look on our hearts as if we were lovers. But it is a wand that is waved only over the hearts of those who believe in Jesus as their Savior. The rest of humanity is out of luck.

Most Catholics say the only way to make up for a heart that is not throbbing with love is to suffer in purgatory, if you are fortunate enough to end up there.

As for me I have no idea how God goes about receiving us. Thanks to my night visitor I do believe that God is an all-needy presence on planet earth courting my love, not as an all-mighty presence banking on threats and promises. An all-needy presence would truly be an incomprehensible mystery. Unfortunately, that kind of presence has been lost in the translation of the mystery, as will be seen in the next meditation.

My Mother The Church:

My night visitor spoke to me by way of my religious imagination. You know as well as I that my night visitor was for the most part me talking to myself. There is nothing wrong with that when done in good grace. But what would Mother Church say about my night visitor? She celebrates the helpless presence of God only at Christmas time – and even then surrounds that helplessness with power stories.

Mother Church (Popes, Bishops, teachers, parishioners, family and many of my colleagues and friends) would say: There is no mystery about how God goes about being God. Judgment day will make that perfectly clear. God will be dressed for court not for courting.

Judaism, Christianity, and Islam agree on two things. Jerusalem will be the location for the Last Judgment. "Guilty" or "Not Guilty" will be God's first and last words, not "Surprise!" The only possible surprise would be if you are a pious Protestant and God wants only pious Catholics, or vice versa.

One look at God on that fateful day and we will feel like fools if we had expected that, like the father of the prodigal son, God will have already killed the fatted calf, will rush to greet us even while we were still far away from heaven's gate. We would be fools to believe that our Father will be unable to restrain his love once he catches sight of us returning to him, true prodigals that we are.

No doubt, my teachers say, it is true that while still in our bodies God does delight in playing the storied lover, as in the stories of the father and his two sons, the shepherd and his lost sheep, and the woman and her lost coin. Until the moment of death God plays the all-needy lover and allows clergy and conscience to play the no-nonsense judge. But that ends with our death. The God who courted us in life will summon us to court in death. His love will no longer be admissible as a defense. His justice is now in play. You may as well forget self-defense, as in "when did I see you hungry?" and pleas of that sort. Why do you think the portrait in the Sistine Chapel is that of God the judge not God the doting father? No question about it. God's first words will be "Guilty" or "Not Guilty" – not "Surprise".

Without a doubt, death is the deadline. The nanosecond after our last breath is payback time not pleading time. The Gospels make that perfectly clear. One criminal used his last breath to console Jesus and the other to curse Jesus. One made the deadline and the other missed it, no pun intended. God could change the deadline, or have no deadline. But God has decided not to do that. And that's that! Death is the deadliest deadline ever conceived. That is what an early Christian writer may have meant when he wrote "…it is an established truth that the flesh is the very condition on which salvation hangs."

Me, myself and I:

Not so fast, I say to my teachers, colleagues, family, friends, bishop and that early Christian writer. Our biblical texts about judgment day can hardly be taken literally. Who takes literally Jesus' parable of the last judgment? If I can't take Jesus' last reference to hell literally I take nothing that is said about hell literally. Why is it that the last parable of Jesus is virtually ignored? You know why as well as I do. It is too frightening to imagine a judgment based on how we treat "the least". That is why you will never hear a sermon warning you that you will be sent to hell if you do not treat them as if they were Jesus. If such sermons were preached there would have to be a sign over heaven's courtroom: "Abandon hope all ye who enter here."

It seems to me that our belief in judgment day flourishes not because of our biblical texts but because of the following human inclinations:

Those who suffer violence, of whom there are so many, believe that divine judgment is payback time. The husband whose beloved wife was raped and murdered can hardly wait for God to get on with sending the brutal bastard to hell.

The wretched and the miserable, of whom there so are many, expect payback for those who had good times at their expense. As Paul Gauguin noted: "Life being what it is we dream of revenge." It is presumed that God dreams our dreams.

The pious and those who think they are pious, of whom there are so many, look forward to the rewards that go with a favorable judgment. Could God have gotten so many of them to obey so many laws and give up so much supposedly sinful pleasure without "his" lures and threats of heaven or hell?

Those who put a great deal of stock in "common sense", of whom there are so many, claim that without a judgment day there would be no justice. Worse yet, without exercising his power to judge, to reward and to punish, God could not hope to maintain order and harmony in the world. Only unlimited divine power can save us from chaos. It is for these reasons that God must be worshiped as the Almighty. Why else would God have unlimited power at his beck and call? Surely it cannot be to save everyone. Not even God can work up a plan that could do that. Could "He"?

But most of all judgment day is trumpeted by the righteous, of whom there are so many. They see this day as garbage-removal day. God sifts out the renegades, the riff-raff, the rabble, and the roughnecks they could never stand to be with – even in heaven. Only by keeping them out on judgment day can God see to it that heaven is truly heavenly. No wonder the righteous see God's holiness as holiness with an attitude. It attacks us rather than embraces us.

I no longer believe it is right and proper that I relate to God as an almighty presence. I will try to defend my disbelief with one long sentence, with a list of "supposes", with some provocative questions, and with a confession of faith.

One long sentence:
In saying my prayers, singing hymns, reciting creeds, and studying about God, my awe of God as an almighty power left little room for living with God as an incomprehensible mystery

as there was nothing mysterious about God's power to make
and to break, to reward and to punish, so much so that whatever
is mysterious about God was of little consequence unless it
related to whether God will accept or reject me, and so I
hesitated to give up praying to God as "almighty" because my
two thousand year old church, rich in wisdom and experience in
these matters, would see my decision as silly or even sinister,
but in a personal act of faith – the kind that is more prominent
among Protestants than Catholics, though I still consider myself
a Catholic – I decided to stop relating to God as "the almighty"
mostly because as I grow closer to meeting God, face to face as
they say, I do expect that the awe of that meeting will be in
seeing "the mystery" not "the might" of God, that is, if love's
power rather than fear's power is what will bind God and me
for all eternity, for it is of the essence of true lovers to reveal to
one another all that is hidden and, on special occasions, it is
their greatest joy to catch the other off guard and cry out:
"Surprise"!, rather than "Submit"!- as is the custom among the
almighty.

My list of supposes:

I know that the image of God as the almighty judge, as the man who goes by the book (though which book is debatable), is deeply embedded in the religious imagination. And yet, I dare to imagine that my return to God may be more like that of the prodigal son to whom the father said "Surprise!" This is a fantasy that sits well with me.

But my fantasy will not displace the sacred and traditional fantasy about being "judged by God". That will never happen in my lifetime, or in yours. I will have to fly to God solo on this one, with the help of the following list of "supposes":

1. Suppose it is God's will to be revered as "the mystery" rather than as "the almighty";

2. Suppose God never spoke one word about "herself" or "her" way of being present on planet earth;

3. Suppose God never gave a verifiable glimpse of the divine mystery to anyone, not even as a burning bush, a cloud, a dove, a transfigured Jesus or a risen Jesus – lest such showing off demean the power and glory of our faith in the mystery;

4. Suppose God's only exception to the rule of being silent and unseen was to speak one word, a word that became living flesh - a Jew living with the Jews;

5. Suppose God's only presence on planet earth is a graceful presence in our hearts, the exact opposite of an almighty presence in heaven – always without anger, always without power moves, always without commands about beliefs and rituals, and never ever as a fist.

6. Suppose God is somehow getting the God-job done, as a smitten lover, and not as a smiting lord, even though most of us suppose otherwise.

Some provocative questions:
1. Since God seems to be touchier about our worship and beliefs than about our behavior which book will God follow in judging us – Jewish, Christian or Muslim? If God follows the Christian book will he follow the Catholic, Protestant, liberal or conservative interpretation?

2. If, before Church law was changed, a pious catholic boy ate a hot dog on Prom night, a Friday, and on the way home was killed instantly in a car crash, did he end up in hell?

As a young man I asked a priest that question. He looked at me as if I were a silly boy asking a stupid question. He said that God would not allow that to happen to a pious boy. I said nothing. But it seemed to me that God is playing a sinister game if he does not allow a good boy to die unrepentant but meanwhile allows his church to scare the hell out of him with its teaching on mortal sin.

3. On judgment day does God say to sinners (whatever "sinner" may mean) "burn in hell" or simply "depart from me"? Both judgments are to be feared but the second less so than the first.

4. Why is the parenting of the almighty not so almighty? Why is it going so badly? What's that all about?

Is it because God relies on poorly run day-care centers called "religions" to do the hands on parenting while he is "at work" running the world? Is it because the children of God are dysfunctional children, thanks to their evil inclinations and weaknesses and to the power of Satan? Is it because we are not really and truly the images and likenesses of God? How could God as an almighty presence do so poorly in relating to his images and likenesses?

5. Why in the last pages of the bible does divine might erupt in apocalyptic fury – as if "his" almighty presence in history did not get the job done? Why does God's Son return to rule with an iron rod? What kind of final solution is that for the all good and all loving Father of all?

6. Why do we still believe that the metaphors of Lord, king and judge reveal God's love as "tough love"? How tough can love be before tough is no longer love? Why should I believe tough love is the best God can do?

7. Is it not now obvious that God as an almighty presence does not mean what the first and last books of the bible tell us it means? Almighty does not mean that God made the world in six days, flooded it in forty days, and will incinerate it in the final days.

8. Why is God as "the all-mystery" given such little attention by our preachers and teachers?

9. In reference to loving God does "love" really mean "obedience"? Is that why are we "commanded" to love the Lord our God? Not even God can command love but God can surely command obedience.

That's exactly what I was taught by the nuns. I was told over and over again that my obedience was proof of my love. That's all the proof of love I needed. The list of rules to be obeyed as proof of love was put in the hands of the Church's official teachers. They could make the list as extensive as they saw fit – and they saw fit. And why not? The bible featured God as very obedience-minded. "He" is featured as Lord not Lover, as a prolific lawmaker, as a judge who goes by the book. To love God was to obey God - or else.

10. If God settled for obedience as love do Catholics have the advantage over the Protestants? We have more to obey than they do. And we have the trappings of authority that constantly reminded us of our duty to obey. Color is one of them. The Pope wears white, the cardinals wear red, the bishops wear

purple and the priests wear black. Added to these colors were their titles: Your holiness, your eminence, your excellency, monsignor, and father.

11. Is the biblical command to love God not what it seems? Is the command to love God more like a kick in the butt than an actual command? Get cracking! You have a long way to go buster before you learn to love God with all your heart, mind and soul. What do you think?

My confession of faith:

I believe it demeans God to suppose "He" keeps a book on my every thought, word and deed and comes at me fist first, as is the custom of the mighty – especially those who want to be renowned for their might.

I believe it is close to blasphemy to claim that divine love woos us mostly by favors and fear; that divine might rather than divine love is the foundation of all that is good – all that is of God.

I believe that calling God "almighty" is not the truest, fairest, and most appropriate way of addressing God. Surely "almighty" cannot mean that God goes with love as "the promise" but relies on might as "the solution." This would be a God made to our image and likeness, rather than the other way round.

I believe that God is not with us as the almighty white guy with a beard. If that's God then I'm Napoleon.

I end this meditation with a note of caution. In picturing God as crying out "surprise" I'm just messing around with the metaphor of God as "all-mystery" in reaction to the metaphor God as "almighty". I am trying to get a feel for that mystery moment- that nanosecond after death. I have no idea what meeting the God will be like – nor do you. In the twilight of my life I am going with "surprise" as God's welcome home greeting. When I die I do not plan to bring with me a pocket full of certainties. When I depart I will not go with the word "God" on my lips –as if it were a proper noun, as if the name itself revealed the mystery.

The Mother of All Mysteries:

The name of God is the mother of all mysteries.

At a peak moment in his life with God Moses slyly asked God to reveal his name. Surely, Moses said to God, Pharaoh will ask me your name when I claim you sent me. Moses, supposedly the shy and stuttering type, was pushing God here. But God was ready for Moses. Just tell old Pharaoh that YHWH sent you. The exact meaning of these four consonants (vowels were not used in the sacred text) is still unclear: "I am"; "I am who I am"; "I will be who I will be"; "I will become who I will become".

Why Moses would ask God to reveal his name made little sense. The God of Israel had long been known by the name 'Shaddai' (the almighty) or by the noun "El" (a divine being in contrast to a human being). When "El" was used for the God of Israel it was usually used in a way that distinguished him from other divine beings: "El" of your Fathers, "El" of Israel, "El" of Jacob. The implication was that Israel's divine being was more powerful than the divine beings of other tribes.

In the Exodus story Moses popped his question just as "Shaddai" (the almighty) was about to play the Godfather in making Egypt an offer it could not refuse. The almighty must have shocked Moses in giving "himself" the name of YHWH – a name that suggests mystery rather than might.

At a peak moment in my life with God I came to favor the translation "I will become who I will become". But lately, in prayer and reflection, I have been favoring my personal translation of YHWH as MYOB (mind your own business). My prayers to MYOB have been going something like this:

It would be great if we would hear from you from time to time. But in minding my own business I go along with you in getting the God-job done in absolute silence.

"He who knows how to keep silent discovers an alphabet that has as many letters as the ordinary one." (???)

It would be a blessing if you would show yourself every so often. But in minding my own business I suppose you know best. I suppose John tells it like you want it to be told.

"No one has ever seen God; if we love one another, God lives in us, and his love is perfected in us." (1 Jn. 4:21)

It would be great if your book and your guys did not condemn doubts and questions, if in minding their own business they agreed with the fictional character in "The Big Sky" who conceded:

"A man can think his mind to a nub and not know anything about God. He's got to die, I reckon, to find out…"

I confess to you, YHWH/MYOB, my deepest regrets: I regret fearing you as an alpha male- as if "to terrorize is divine"; I regret relating to you as a touchy teacher – as if "to err is unforgivable"; I regret craving assurances – as if signs and wonders are the foundation of faith.

Thanks YHWH/MYOB, for the gift of a long life. I rejoice as did a beloved fictional Archbishop "...I am enjoying to the full that period of reflection which is the happiest conclusion to a life of action." Thank you most of all for giving me the many years it has taken to learn to love you as "the mystery" - and for letting me end my days with another mission, one that gave me new life.

My mission, if I can find a publisher, is to remind my readers that our preachers' sermons and teachers' bible stories about God's almighty presence have made mince meat of the belief that God is present to us as an incomprehensible mystery. You know what mince meat is. It is a mixture that looks like meat, may have some meat in it, but is not meat. There is not much meat left in "the mystery" once "the almighty" is added to the mix.

My faith community and me:

Yes, Yes, Jim, say what you like but you know very well that staying alive spiritually means to live off the myths, customs, beliefs, and structures of one's faith community. Living on planet earth is a social enterprise for those who believe in God – and very much so for your faith community.

I know, I know, I know that only too well. I know the grace of community. But I believe my faith community was conceived in the womb of Israel; is Judaism's twin. Paul found it hard to make sense of these twins. It was the occasion for him expressing his awe about the unsearchable and inscrutable ways of God in dealing with communities. Where there is a faith community there are always questions about the grace of community. See Romans 11: 33-34.

I know I am taking a risk in my solo flight. But leaving this planet is a solitary enterprise. I can take no one with me – not the Pope, not the bible. God will not ask: "Jim, who does your Church say that I am? God will ask: "Jim, who do you say that I am?" God will not be expecting the correct answer. God knows that no human answer can be correct. But God will be expecting my answer. God gave me my faith as a gift. What I have done with that gift is what concerns God. God will be looking for what I have come to believe not what I was taught to believe.

I cannot go on living with the image of God favored by my community. I cannot do this without fear of offending God. For me, old age is "the great grey grace" of my life. It is giving me time to make peace with what I truly believe. It has given me time to go with my conscience. It has given me time to work out my death-bed prayer:

There is no God but G?????. Praise G????? from whom
All blessings flow. How they flow we will never know.
If there is any value to what I write about G?????
as incomprehensible mystery, that alone is worth the
price of my book.

15. FROM HERE TO ETERNITY -

?????????????????????????

"Life is a great surprise. I do not see why
death should not be an even greater one."
    Vladimir Nabokov

"When I was young, I was extremely scared of
dying. But now I think it is a very wise
arrangement. It's like a light that is extinguished.
Not very much to make a fuss about."
    Ingmar Bergman

In reflecting on the after life (whatever that may mean) I take
heart in a story told by a Russian novelist. It went something
like this:
    A woman, rich, Russian and regal, was stopped
    by St. Peter at the pearly gates. He saw no
    reason to admit her and sent her to hell.
    The insult angered her more than anything.
    She raised such a fuss there that Satan begged
    Peter for a second opinion. Tell her to give me

one act of kindness said Peter, anything, no
matter how insignificant and I will remove her
from hell. Peter was just about to give up when
Satan sent word that she once gave an onion to a
beggar. Good enough said Peter. He sent an angel
to hell with an onion. Hold onto the onion the angel
said and I will pull you out of hell. She held and he
pulled. When the others saw what was happening they
grabbed onto her and soon hell was in danger of
being depopulated. But the rich woman looked back
and shouted, let go, that's my onion. All, including
the rich woman, fell back into hell.

This Russian story may sound like bleeding-heart theology to
some. But we need stories like this to confront a hard-hearted
theology. If my church can suppose one act of masturbation can
put us in hell it is not out of line to suppose one onion can put
us in heaven. Indeed, if all persons entering eternity are stamped
"image and likeness of God" this story is not out of line, other
than in allowing for a hell.

This story of a providential onion came to be experienced by me in a most unexpected way. You won't believe this but in December of 2004 I received an "onion" pulling me back to Rome where I had lived and studied for six happy years. The "onion" was an invitation from a Cardinal who was ordained with me on December 8, 1954. He graciously spent three weeks trying to locate me. He looked for me, he found me, and he invited me to Rome – even though he knew I was no longer functioning as a priest. He invited me to share with him and two Roman pastors (the last name of one pastor means "little onion") the celebration of our ordination. It was a week I shall never forget. I had traveled far from my traditional roots but returned to Rome without feeling like a stranger.

Two years after I was pulled back to Rome by a "Cardinal Onion" an "Easter Monday Onion" pulled me into the mystery of mysteries.

As my body was basking in the marvelous rays of the sun and digesting the ruins of a meatball sandwich I thought I heard the voice of Jesus. I do not know whether I was in my basking and digesting body or out of my basking and digesting body. Only God knows. Since I am no St. Paul I started to dismiss what I thought I was hearing. It is just the sun and the sandwich stirring up my imagination. But, as you well know, I believe the imagination is the God-spot of the mind. So I decided to let the voice have its say.

Jesus: "Jim, you did the best you could in writing about the mystery of my thirty years in hiding. I truly appreciate your efforts. I knocked myself out living as a marginal man rather than as a mighty Messiah. It was not easy living most of my life as a non-entity rather than as someone to be reckoned with. It pains me that Christianity dismisses this fact so easily and gorges itself on stories of me as 'the Christ'.

And you did the best you could in writing about the mystery of my crucifixion. Christians love the bloody nails that pinned me to the cross. They believe them to be the keys that opened heaven. I loathe those bloody nails. I know that they cut my mission short. I know I could have made more of a difference given the time. Why else would I die crying out like a Godforsaken wretch? My mission was to renew the face of planet earth. My hands and feet were the tools of my trade. Nailing them to the cross brought my mission to a dead halt. If the face of the earth has not been renewed by now you can figure it out for yourself.

Thank you, Jim, for linking my thirty hidden years and my three hours on the cross to what many believe to be 'mission impossible' on planet earth. But don't expect any book endorsement from me. I don't do endorsements. Your book will rise or fall on its own merits.

But you do have a friend in Jesus. I will walk with you from here to eternity. That's my word. I'm sticking to it."

My Easter Monday Jesus may be a fantasy.

But if G????? and Son are an incomprehensible mystery then faith in them rightly feeds on such fantasies. If this incomprehensible mystery is a mystery of infinite love then faith rightly feeds on fantasies of great expectations. As a near-death man of faith my fantasy no longer features angels leading me to paradise, or pearly gates at its entrance, or St. Peter with the keys to the gates. When I try to visualize my death I see only Jesus. He is waiting to escort me into the mystery. I imagine going from here to eternity as being something like this:

Jesus: Let's get moving old buddy. It's a long way to
    Tipperary. It's a long, long way.

Jim: Thanks for the "old buddy" and for the Tipperary
    quip, and for telling me this will not be a quick
    trip. I have a lot of questions I want to ask you:

    Am I really and truly an image and likeness of God?
    I still cannot imagine how that could be.
    I'll believe it when I see it.

    Will I get my old body back or will I get one of
    those spiritual bodies Paul wrote about?
    If I do get my La Croce body back
    will there be any sex in heaven?
    You said there would be no marriage in heaven
    but that was a put-down answer to a trick question.
    No one has given me a definite "no" on sex.
    Will I have my 30 year old body as the nuns
    taught me or the body I die with?
    Will babies have baby bodies in heaven?

Am I going to live with God forever – and ever?
How would that work? The very thought scares me.

If God is all knowing, all loving, and all-mighty
why would he create anyone "He" knows will
so abuse his free will that he will end up in hell?
By the way, is there a hell?
The claim there is a hell scared the hell out of
me for most of my life.

Have my rude awakenings offended Your Father?
Is he as touchy and testy as advertised?
Should I be nervous about this following a wide awake-
dream I had not so long ago?:

I was about to cross a busy street.
I was in my body and yet out of my body.
A Mack truck had tried to kill a child.
I saw God leaning over her trembling body.
I heard the child scream at God:
You should have anticipated this.
I don't want to die. I'm too young to die.

Don't let me die. God almighty, don't let me die.

Without thinking I screamed into her scream:

I will not let you die. I will kill God if you die.

She looked into my eyes. She knew that I meant it.

She believed I could do it.

Hell, I believed I could do it.

Meanwhile, God was screaming into my scream:

While you are at it there are a few other

images besides "almighty" you should take down.

The girl looked at me and at God and went to sleep.

Whether it was the sleep of death I cannot say.

But I don't believe God took my threat lightly.

Jesus, you know my day-dream is more than a dream.

You know what's in my book.

Will your Father hold my dream and book against me?

Jesus: What fools ye mortals be. What kind of a

    God do you think my Father is?

    Think Nazarene, not Nazi. Get real!

There are a few other images of my father
that should be taken down.

Jim: Okay, okay, I get it. Think mystery not almighty.
Think loving not lording. Case closed!

But one last question, please.
My granddaughter asked me to ask you this.
I promised her that I would do so.
Is it your will that women should never be
priests, bishops, and popes?

Jesus: Jim, what do you think?
Women image God as well as men.
A woman's "yes" gave me my flesh, real flesh
not bread-flesh.
Two women told the men where to go if they want to
see me as the resurrected Christ.

Hell no, it is not my will.
Jeez Louise, Jim, stop it with the questions.
You'll know everything soon enough.

Stop worrying. And stop fidgeting.

You are driving me crazy.

Jim: O.K., O.K., are we there yet?

Jesus, Mary, and Holy St. Joseph!!!

How long is this trip going to take?

Jesus: Jim!!! Are you taking my name in vain?

Are you trying to cover it up by adding

the names of Mary and Joseph?

Jim: Jesus! How could you even......oh my G!!!!!!

??? The Beginning ???

What do I know?

Faith, Hope and Love do not trump Mystery